RENDEZVOUS AT MIDWAY
U.S.S. *Yorktown* and the Japanese Carrier Fleet

Books by Pat Frank

ALAS, BABYLON MR. ADAM
AN AFFAIR OF STATE
HOLD BACK THE NIGHT

By Joseph D. Harrington

THE KAITEN WEAPON:
(*with Yutaka Yokota*)
The Story of Japan's Human Torpedoes

Rendezvous

U.S.S. *YORKTOWN* AND THE

by Pat Frank and

Forewords by ADMIRAL FRANK JACK FLETCHER

(UNITED STATES NAVY, *retired*)

The John Day Company,

at Midway

JAPANESE CARRIER FLEET

Joseph D. Harrington

and YAHACHI TANABE

Former Commander, IMPERIAL JAPANESE NAVY

Illustrated

New York

Copyright © 1967 by Joseph D. Harrington

Library of Congress Catalogue
Card Number: 67-10829

Acknowledgments

★ ★ ★ ★ ★ ★ ★

★ ★ ★ First thanks must go to Lieutenant Commanders Dave Cooney, Frank Steele, and Dan Dagle at the Navy Department for their almost daily assistance over a twenty-month research period. Master Chief Personnelman Edward Morosky and Yeoman Harry Buckingham provided invaluable leads and information for hundreds of letters and interviews. Mrs. Mildred Mayeux, longtime friend of one of the authors, gave them the same total cooperation and attitude of interest she gives all writers who use the Navy's operational archives.

Especially appreciated is the contribution made by Professor Thaddeus Tuleja, whose scholarly research and lucid writing style have given readers the best account of the Midway battle in print. Professor Tuleja graciously made available to the authors some of his own personal research papers.

The editors of the *United States Naval Institute Proceedings* gave permission to use material originally appearing their publication.

The book could not have been written, nonetheless, without an outpouring of information from many hundreds of other people, who took the time to write letters, dictate tape recordings of their recollections, refer the authors to innumerable additional sources of information, or endure lengthy interviews. In addition to those whose names appear in these pages, the authors are especially indebted to Frank J. Baldino, John S. Barnett, Charles C. Barr, Floyd H. Bennett, Demetrio Bernal, Philip R. Blouin, Jules Bodenschatz, Thomas S. Brent, Judson Brodie, Raymond G. Carlson, Joseph G. Chartier, Benjamin F. Coopman, Arthur W. Deike, Glyn G. Dillard, Eugene Domienik, Joseph Fazio, Dail Fine, Bernard H. Forsting, Eugene R. Fortney, Arthur L. Foster, Robert Good, Jr., Paul W. Grubbs, Harry and Robert Grunow, Edwin C. Haywood, Edward H. Hermanson, Clark L. Hertenstein, Louis B. Hess, Jr., Nelson M. Hollandsworth, August W. Hovland, Ellis F. Jackson, Arthur G. Jacobs, Elton Jardell, Lawrence M. Jarley, Irvin A. Jaworski, Edwin G. Johnson, Dale C. Jones, Michael "Kaply" Kaplyawka, Dennis A. Kelly, Ludwig Koschak, Raymond O. Lewis, William R. Lewis, George E. Lillicotch, Stanford E. Linzey, Jr., Charles P. Lunn, Clyde G. McClure, Thomas J. McGann, Kenneth A. McIntosh, Albert F. Medley, Eldridge S. Mitchell, Jr., Peter Montalvo, Tivis Newberry, Robert R. Newcomb, Earnest E. Parton, Dr. Joseph P. Pollard, Robert Ready, Orville L. Ritchie, Duane E. Robertson, Donald R. Root, Robert J. Rudek, Louis Rulli, Tom Rush, Edward B. Smolenski, Howard C. Stein, Melvin C. Stiller, John J. Strong, Dale L. Stuart, John L. Tallman, Oliver C. Thore, Bernard F. Verboncouer, V. F. Wadsworth, Harold C. Weaver, Elwood R. Wilson, Maurice E. Witting, Bryan C. Woods, Bob S. Wray, George A. Wright, George H. Wright, James S. Xanders, Doyle Yates, Robert

H. Zander, and countless others who telephoned or passed on information in conversations.

I hope our efforts merit theirs.

JOSEPH D. HARRINGTON

Bowie, Maryland, 1966

*A section of illustrations from photo-
graphs appears following page 128.*

Foreword

★ ★ ★ ★ ★ ★ ★

★ ★ ★ The war was only a few weeks old when I took my flag and my staff aboard U.S.S. *Yorktown* at San Diego, and our situation in the Pacific was indeed unhappy. Hong Kong and Wake had fallen. The two British battleships on which we had counted so much for stopping a Japanese southward advance had been sunk off Malaya. Allied strength in the western Pacific was but a handful of cruisers, some destroyers, and a few submarines, no match at all for the onrushing Japanese fleet.

The Philippines had been invaded at many points. General Douglas MacArthur had declared Manila an open city and was moving his forces into the Bataan Peninsula. There, as the war plans ordered, he was to fight as long as he could, then retreat into Fortress Corregidor and wait for us in California and Hawaii to come to his aid.

We could give no help, of course. The battleships that were to crash through the central Pacific and combine with the British and Dutch forces against the Japanese lay in the mud of Pearl Harbor. The Japanese warlords, on the last day of 1941, were free to strike wherever it pleased them to do so.

Few persons recognized then, or remember now, how grand the Japanese strategy was and how close it came to being realized. Japan struck east in early December, immobilizing the main strength of the U.S. fleet with a surprise attack on Pearl Harbor. She was now striking south, to control or isolate Australia, the only logical place from which a great counterattack could be launched against her.

She was also getting ready to strike west, across India, and into the Near East, joining up with German forces under General Rommel in Africa.

A look at the globe will awe anyone who considers just how much of the world the Rome-Berlin-Tokyo Axis would have controlled had its master plan been successful. Hitler's troops at that time, remember, were enjoying success everywhere. They seemed well on their way to complete victory in Europe and in North Africa.

With Japanese victories, the Axis Powers would have held the great Eurasian landmass, with all its wealth and resources, the world island. America would have been isolated and dealt with at leisure.

In the Pacific Ocean, at the beginning of 1942, the United States had no means whatever of thwarting Japanese plans except for small task forces built around four aircraft carriers—*Enterprise, Saratoga, Lexington,* and *Yorktown.* A fifth carrier, *Hornet,* would soon be on its way from the Atlantic. So it was that the carrier task force was thrust into war.

Our aircraft carriers had to perform two tasks: protect what holdings we still had, and keep the Japanese fleet off-balance and dispersed by widely scattered, sudden attacks on enemy holdings. We had to keep this up until replacement and supplementary warships could be constructed, until America's industrial might could make itself felt. And Lord help us if the Japanese fleet ever assembled against us, outnumbered as we were.

I had the privilege of commanding American sailors in two great carrier battles of the Pacific—Coral Sea and Midway. The first battle saved Australia and marked a new experience for the Japanese fleet, retreat. The second battle broke the back of Japan's naval air arm, with four of her best aircraft carriers going down and hundreds of her best pilots lost.

In both battles, I fought from the bridge of U.S.S. *Yorktown*, a fine ship, with whose officers and men it was an honor to serve. The full contribution of *Yorktown* men to America's success in the Pacific has never been revealed until now. Security precautions kept it secret at the time it happened, and later happenings in the war, when we were obviously on the road to victory, overshadowed it. After the war, when all the facts became available and were cleared for release, they were not reported fully. Certain myths were repeated so often that they became accepted truths.

The authors of this book decided to tell *Yorktown's* story. They gathered and documented all the facts obtainable concerning her, then assembled the personal experiences of men who sailed in *Yorktown*, so that her story could be told in their words. When I was first approached for an interview, I was impressed with the wealth of information, some of it new even to me, that these gentlemen possessed. I was also impressed with their meticulous method of cross-checking every bit of information. I remain impressed with the final result of their work.

U.S.S. *Yorktown* was in the thin line of aircraft carriers which were all we had to deter the Japanese with until our forces were built up. She helped keep the enemy spread out. When he finally did concentrate his forces for attack, she and her men helped meet and defeat them.

Once the Japanese Navy lost four aircraft carriers at Midway, it lost its momentum and never recovered it. Australia was never threatened again. Nor was Hawaii. America was able to divert men and resources to Africa, England, and Europe, to stop Hitler, and to send others to Burma and India to assist in stopping the Japanese there. Victory became a matter of time.

Aircraft carriers like *Yorktown* added a new dimension to naval warfare. They guarded supply lines, hunted down enemy submarines, protected convoys and even their own escorting capital ships, beat off enemy air counterattacks, softened up beaches for invasion, and rained destruction on enemy cities. They became an integral part, indeed the core, of our naval power. They remain so today. As I write this, they are off Vietnam, demonstrating their unique ability to apply as much or as little force as is necessary in backing up the foreign policy of the United States.

What carriers can do we first learned in ships like U.S.S. *Yorktown,* during the tough, trying days of early 1942. The battle lessons of Coral Sea and Midway were applied with ever-increasing effectiveness later—with such effectiveness, in fact, that we were able to reduce our pilot training program radically in 1944. Our pilots were so well trained and superior to the enemy by that time that their losses were far below combat expectations.

Most *Yorktown* men lived through Coral Sea and Midway. Badly outnumbered in the war's early days, they fought bravely and survived. They then trained and led others in the ways of victory. I am pleased to know that, at last, their story is being told in detail, just as it happened.

FRANK JACK FLETCHER
U.S. Navy Admiral (Retired)

Araby, La Plata, Maryland, 1966

Foreword

★ ★ ★ ★ ★ ★ ★

★ ★ ★ Before World War II, in the Japanese Navy, our submarine strategy was similar to that of the American Navy. Submarine commanders were essentially attack scouts. Their chief targets were to be enemy capital ships—battleships, aircraft carriers, and cruisers.

If war threatened, our finest submarines were to lie off enemy anchorages. When the enemy sailed out against Japan, they were to attack him at once, and many times again along his route of advance. He would also be met by long-range submarines from our home ports. Such attacks, theoretically, would reduce the enemy fleet's strength to the point where our own main body, on meeting the enemy, would destroy what was left of his naval forces. Japan would be preserved.

Once the Pacific naval war started, the United States abandoned this strategy. American submarines concentrated their attacks on Japan's merchant shipping, with great effect. As the years passed, they reduced the supply of materials coming into our homeland to a trickle, then almost cut it off completely. Our nation was left helpless. We ran out of materials with which to make war.

Japanese submarine strategy, however, did not change. Our boats were continually ordered to attack American capital ships, which soon learned to cope with us. Our submarines were almost always beaten off or sunk. As the war went against us and it became too late to attack the Allied merchant marine, Japanese submarines were used as supply transports and finally for suicide missions, sending away *kaiten* (human torpedoes) against the ever-growing American fleet. After the first six months of war our submarines made very few attacks on enemy merchant ships.

We started the war with a very fine submarine force, then wasted it. More than 100 boats and many thousands of trained men were lost, with very little real damage to the enemy to show for this terrible waste.

My participation in the Midway battle was one of the high points in the war for Japanese submarines. It was also the high point of my naval career and of my life. I have relived many times what is told in these pages, always with pride and wonder.

One of the authors interviewed me. The story of my submarine at Midway, *I-168*, is included here. I hope that readers will recognize the bravery and loyalty of the men who followed me into battle, obeying my orders at once and unflinchingly. Of such men are great navies composed.

Many of my Midway crewmen died in later battles and are now honored at Yasukuni Shrine, in Tokyo. I will always honor them in my heart.

YAHACHI TANABE
Former Commander
Imperial Japanese Navy

Tokyo, Japan, 1966

RENDEZVOUS AT MIDWAY

Prologue

★ ★ ★ ★ ★ ★ ★

★ ★ ★ The Roosevelts had always been good to the United States Navy. Teddy built the modern Navy and sent its stubby battleships around the world to show what wonders he had wrought. Franklin collected weathered old naval prints—*Constitution* versus *Guerrière, Wasp* versus *Reindeer, Enterprise* versus *Boxer*—became Secretary of the Navy, and, as President of the United States, through the Vinson-Trammel Act of 1934, gave new meaning to history; he stepped up naval construction and, none too soon, built the ships that stood off Japan in the desperate early months of World War II.

It was, of course, still a battleship Navy. American yards, in those balmy prewar days, were building, at prodigious expense, the 35,000-tonners—*North Carolina, Washington, Indiana, Massachusetts, Alabama,* and *South Dakota.* Later they would begin building the 45,000-tonners—*Iowa, New Jersey, Missouri,* and *Wisconsin.*

> Like most weapons of destruction created in times of peace, [Richard Hough has written] the first function of the battleship was to instill fear in the hearts of men. . . .

21

No instrument of war has ever surpassed the battleship in its menacing grandeur, or in its disastrous ability to condition man's mind to the destruction of his fellows. And yet, for all the sacrifices, the passions, the political manipulations and pressures it occasioned, the battleship was scarcely ever used in combat.

It was scarcely to be used in combat in World War II and not to be used at all in the role its admirers had envisioned, in the great fleet-to-fleet encounters where the future of the world would hang in the balance.

There is nothing very menacing about an aircraft carrier's appearance. It carries no great guns; it is simply a floating airfield, its superstructure pushed to one side to give its airplanes a full deck for landing and taking off. But in World War II, in the vast stretches of the Pacific Ocean, the carrier was to be America's ultimate weapon.

Statistics tell part of the story. America went to war in 1941 with 19 battleships and only 7 carriers. It emerged victorious in 1945 with more than 100 carriers and only 24 battleships. Even today, in the advancing years of the age of atomic weaponry, giant carriers roam the seas off the coast of Vietnam. America's three remaining battleships— *Missouri*, *Iowa*, and *Wisconsin*—bob gently at dockside, neglected and forgotten.

This is the story of an aircraft carrier. Her name was *Yorktown*, third of her line* in the U.S. Navy. Her wartime career spanned only 182 days, but they were days (and

* The first *Yorktown*, launched in 1839, was a 566-ton 16-gun sloop of war. In 1850, while attached to the African Squadron, she was wrecked on one of the Cape Verde Islands. The second *Yorktown*, a clumsy 1,710-ton gunboat, was launched in 1888 and compiled a wholly undistinguished record. She was sold out of the service in 1921.

nights) of wild and deadly combat. In *Yorktown's* brief and stormy career, she compiled a record of almost unparalleled glory. Yet for all she accomplished, history has dealt with her shabbily. Gallantry and a thirst for truth require that her virtue be defended.

Yorktown's story begins with her birth, for ships, like people, are born. *Yorktown* was christened on April 4, 1936, at the Naval Operating Base, Norfolk, Virginia. There, in the same port where Teddy Roosevelt had waved farewell to his coal-burning Great White Fleet as it began its voyage around the world, another Roosevelt, Eleanor, wife of the Commander in Chief, splashed the traditional champagne across her bows. "I christen thee *Yorktown*," she said.

Yorktown—a ship her men nostalgically called Old Yorky —thus became the nation's fifth aircraft carrier. The first, *Langley*, an ungainly converted collier, joined the fleet in 1922. *Lexington* and *Saratoga*, immense 33,000-tonners, were commissioned as carriers in 1927; both had been designed as battle cruisers. The fourth carrier, *Ranger*, was the first this nation built from the keel up as an aircraft carrier. Only 14,500 tons, she joined the Navy in 1934. *Yorktown* was next. Then, not many months later, along came *Enterprise*, her sister ship. *Hornet*, so similar to *Yorktown* and *Enterprise* that she was almost a sister ship, was completed only six weeks before the war began.

These, then, were the carriers with which America went to war. One of them, *Langley*, had been converted to an aircraft transport with practically no flight deck; she was useless. The burden had to be carried by *Yorktown, Enterprise, Wasp, Hornet, Ranger, Lexington,* and *Saratoga*. And in the early months of the war in the Pacific almost the entire burden fell on four ships—*Yorktown, Enterprise, Hornet,* and *Lexington.*

War, in those days following *Yorktown's* commissioning, seemed wildly improbable. For *Yorktown,* in her early years, the greatest enemy was boredom. A poem that appeared in the ship's newspaper, the *Yorktown Crier,* on January 13, 1940, thus summed things up:

> Now here I stand and stand some more,
> This job's by now a beastly bore.
> My muscles ache, my feet are sore,
> Why, I'd lots rather be at war.

Life, for the men of *Yorktown,* was indeed a bore, but it was not exactly a hardship. An article in the program published on the occasion of *Yorktown's* commissioning described what life aboard the new ship would be like; it sounded almost idyllic. The anonymous author wrote:

> To start their days, there won't be a boatswain's mate shouting "Up all hammocks" in their ears, or a bugle poking down a hatch to blow them out of their bunks; it will all be done with the aid of loudspeakers. . . . And all of the crew will sleep in metal bunks; there will be no hammocks or cots used.
>
> There will be no main deck to scrub down with salt water and sand. The flight deck is stained red and aside from sweeping and an occasional new coat of stain it needs no attention.

Breakfast, the author continued, would be served cafeteria-style, and everyone would have a chance to read local newspapers (or the radio press when at sea). Yorktowners would not even have to polish the brightwork, for the fittings were stainless steel. "A fast wipe with a damp cloth, and 'Presto!' it's done."

Often, lunch would be followed by a band concert on the hangar deck. Later, perhaps, the crew would be allowed to play basketball or even softball. "On this ship, there should be no reason to curtail recreation because of cramped quarters."

Then, before dinner, if ice cream looked better than the regular meal, "there is a soda fountain aboard, stocked with all sorts of good things to eat." After dinner, the author went on, the crew would be able to browse in the library or play acey-deucey in the recreation room. Then, topping off the day, movies would be shown every night starting at seven-thirty.

Even in peacetime, life aboard *Yorktown* would never be quite as easy as this prophet suggested. There was, after all, work to be done; American sailors did receive their share of valuable training. But as the article implied, Americans in 1940 were not thinking about going to war. And the American Navy was not eagerly preparing for it.

With the Japanese, things were different. The Japanese Navy, man for man, was better trained than the U.S. Navy. Japanese ships were just as well built as American ships; many were superior to their American counterparts. Japanese battleships, for example, were 50 percent faster than their American counterparts.

American ships maneuvered in the Caribbean, off Pearl Harbor, and off San Diego, in warm, placid waters. The Japanese Navy maneuvered off its own stormy shores and in and around the Kurile Islands. A famous Japanese admiral in the 1930's, Nobumasa Suetsugu, was nicknamed "Seven Days" because he kept his ships and his men working around the clock, week in and week out. Saburo Sakai, the fighter pilot who shot down American hero Colin Kelly in the opening days of the war, said that some Japanese sailors could not take the pressure; they committed suicide by jumping overboard. Juzo Mori, a torpedo plane pilot who sank the battleship *California* at Pearl Harbor, pointed out that he and other Japanese pilots flew twelve hours every day for three months before Pearl Harbor—four hours in the morning, four hours in the afternoon, four hours at night. "We lost," he reported, "large numbers of planes and pilots." In the two years preceding the start of war, the Japanese lost three submarines by collision during high-speed maneuvers.

During all this time the American Navy operated under the strictest economy measures. Training was actually cut back in 1938 because American ships had used up more than their allotment of fuel in July, 1937, searching for Amelia Earhart, the famous aviatrix. Equally typical was the refusal of the Navy Department to allow U.S. ships to fire live torpedoes.

The Japanese were thinking war. They had gone to war with China in 1937. Bombing attacks against the Chinese mainland had been launched from the carriers *Ryujo, Kaga,* and *Hosho.* Japanese naval aviators had become the most highly practiced in the world.

It was an old story with the Japanese. They had bought their first warplanes in Europe prior to 1914. Their experimentations were so intense that one expert contends that all of Japan's pioneer airmen had been killed by 1916. All kinds of people gave them a hand. An American gave Japan 90,000 dollars in 1919 for "the purchase of flying machines and the training of pilots." Great Britain, in 1923, sent a mission of its naval pilots to Japan, to teach and to be taught.

As early as 1915, Admiral Isoroku Yamamoto had predicted that "the most important ship of the future will carry airplanes." And as he saw things, those airplanes would carry torpedoes. In the utmost secrecy the Japanese had developed the torpedo that its ships and airplanes would employ with great effectiveness in the opening months of World War II. It was the finest torpedo of its kind in the world.

Japanese torpedo airplanes were almost as advanced and, by 1936, were able to reach a maximum speed of 240 miles an hour. In 1939 an improved type was capable of speeds up to 300 miles an hour. The American equivalent, the Douglas Devastator, was no match for it, and one day the men who flew them would pay a terrible price for the difference.

The Zero fighter plane being produced by the Japanese in 1940 had a maximum speed of 320 miles an hour, could climb at a rate of 3,000 feet a minute, and could range 500 miles from land bases and return. The American equivalent, the Grumman F4F Wildcat, was inferior to it.

The Japanese dive bomber, the Val, was equally successful. It was faster than its American counterpart, the Douglas SBD Dauntless, and it could carry twice the bombload. Moreover, Japanese pilots had flown their Vals in actual combat.

Japan, to be sure, still had its big battleships, in fact, the biggest battleships ever built. Like other navies, the Imperial Japanese Navy was torn by the argument between the advocates of air power and the defenders of big guns. Still, while the argument droned on, Japan would do more to develop its naval air power than any other nation. When World War II began, the Japanese had ten aircraft carriers, three more than the United States possessed, and if these ships were in some respects possibly inferior to the big American carriers, their planes, their torpedoes, and their personnel were almost surely superior.

Yorktown would come to know this enemy and perish in the knowing. The men of *Yorktown* would come one day to hate the enemy and respect him. But in those peacetime years, to the sailors spooning ice cream at *Yorktown*'s soda bar, war always seemed impossibly remote.

Chapter One

★ ★ ★ ★ ★ ★ ★

★ ★ ★ On December 7, 1941, *Yorktown* lay moored to Pier 7 at the Norfolk naval base. In four years she had come a long way. There had been maneuvers off Cuba in 1939. Later in the same year, after Japan had seized Hainan and Spratly Island, she had raced through the Panama Canal to reinforce the Pacific fleet. It was in the same year, too, that she received the only major overhaul she would ever get, at Bremerton, Washington.

In 1940 she was ordered from the Pacific to the Atlantic, transiting the Panama Canal disguised as *Wasp*. The disguise (all the nameplates were changed) would confuse spies, the Navy reasoned. In those days of tenuous American neutrality, *Yorktown* was used to escort convoys across the Atlantic and to guard against submarines. Perhaps it was not declared war, but the men of *Yorktown* could hardly forget that two U.S. Navy ships, the destroyer *Reuben James* and the tanker *Salinas*, had been sunk by German submarines not far off American shores.

When *Wasp*, the carrier *Yorktown* had pretended to be, was finally "shaken down" and ready to handle her share of defense duties in the Atlantic, *Yorktown* was permitted to put into Norfolk for a routine refit.

On that infamous Sunday, *Yorktown*, secured to the pier by ten Manila lines and two wire cables, had been in port for five of the ninety days that had been allotted to her for reconditioning.

Because it was a Sunday, and a peacetime Sunday at that, most of her crew was ashore, either on leave or on liberty. The airplanes from *Yorktown*'s four squadrons were also ashore, parked at newly completed East Field.

It was 1:20 P.M., Norfolk time, when Commander Mitsuo Fuchida of the Imperial Japanese Navy signaled 183 airplanes to begin the attack on the great U.S. naval base at Pearl Harbor. It was 1:30 P.M. in Norfolk when Lew Godfrey, a twenty-year-old seaman on watch in *Yorktown*'s radio shack, picked up an official message preceded by the high-priority call letters O O O. "Air raid Pearl Harbor," it said. "This is no drill." Godfrey copied it on his typewriter and, clutching the flimsies in his hand, raced down seven ladders from his post high in *Yorktown*'s superstructure to officers' country, where he knew he would find Lieutenant Commander Clarence "Jug" Ray, *Yorktown*'s communications officer. Commander Ray took one look at the message and, with Seaman Godfrey at his side, ran to the quarterdeck to alert Lieutenant Elgin Hurlbert, the OOD (officer of the deck) and, as such, with the ship's captain ashore, commander of *Yorktown*.

Yorktown's skipper, Captain Elliott Buckmaster, whose career was later to be clouded by what history has held was a precipitous decision to abandon his ship, was spending the weekend ashore with his wife at the Ghent Hotel.

Yorktown's executive officer, Commander Joseph "Jocko" Clark, flying on official business from Norfolk to Jacksonville, Florida, was also out of touch.

Lieutenant Hurlbert—whose fellow officers called him Oxy after his alma mater, Occidental College—was shocked by the news from Pearl Harbor. His first action was to order the boatswain's mate of the watch to broadcast news of the attack over *Yorktown's* public-address system. He then sent messengers belowdecks to make sure the duty engineering officer, the duty gunnery officer, and the acting heads of the ship's other departments had got the word. Finally, he doubled the ship's guard as a precaution against sabotage and lined Pier 7 with armed sailors. Boats filled with Marine sharpshooters were lowered to cover the side of the ship facing open water. Satisfied that he had done everything that he could on board, Hurlbert telephoned Captain Buckmaster.

He had just hung up when he received a call from Leroy Gill, an electrician's mate, who, half-asleep in the battery room, had only dimly heard the public-address announcement.

"Who's the wise guy, Mr. Hurlbert?" Gill asked.

"Some Japanese admiral," Hurlbert replied curtly.

At first almost no one on board could believe the news. One member of *Yorktown's* crew stuck his head into CPO (chief petty officer) quarters, where Chief Torpedoman Bob Powell and a dozen others were napping, and shouted, "Hey, you gents, the Japs just bombed Pearl Harbor!" Chief Powell and two or three others threw shoes in the direction of the intruder.

Aerographer Joe Doiron was not a bit surprised. He got

the news from Seaman Godfrey as Godfrey was racing down the ladders to officers' country. "Gil was right," Doiron said later to Seaman Harry Whidden, his companion in the aerology shack. By Gil he meant his brother, Gilbert, a veteran of the Asiatic Fleet, who had been predicting for years that one day Japan and the United States would go to war. But Gil had not lived to see that day. He had been one of those who had died when the destroyer *Reuben James* had gone down in the Atlantic thirty-seven days earlier.

Up on the quarterdeck, Lieutenant Hurlbert reflected on what the news meant to him and to his ship. He had been with *Yorktown* for nine months, and his first appearance aboard the carrier had been memorable. Anxious to make a good appearance, he had stridden up to Captain Buckmaster, clicked his heels, and tossed off a salute that a British Grenadier would have envied.

The captain had returned the salute in the spirit in which it had been rendered, and the game—heel clicking and all —had continued thereafter each time the two men met formally. But on December 7, when Captain Buckmaster came striding up the gangway, the game was over. The salutes were perfunctory, and they would be from that moment on. Buckmaster reviewed the steps Hurlbert had taken, confirmed each of them, and then began issuing orders of his own. He instructed the engine room to light off the boilers and to make preparations for getting *Yorktown* under way. He told Hurlbert to recall all the officers and key enlisted men, and he ordered the reloading of *Yorktown's* airplanes.

Captain Buckmaster, a veteran with twenty-nine years'

service, felt that he must get *Yorktown* ready for action. Perhaps, he thought to himself, the Japanese attack was part of a larger offensive; perhaps the Germans were on the move, too. If *Yorktown* was to fight, she needed sea room.

The captain was an unusual officer. He had spent most of his career in the big-gun Navy and had, in fact, served on six different battleships. Yet in 1936 he was able to realize the potential of air power, a singular mental breakthrough for a man of his background. And so, at the age of forty-seven, he took flight training and won his wings. He had joined *Yorktown*, as skipper, in February, 1941.

One of the first officers to return to *Yorktown* was Lieutenant Commander Jack Delaney, the chief engineer. Delaney had been dozing on a sofa in the apartment his wife, Barbara, had rented just twenty-four hours earlier when he heard the first news flash about Pearl Harbor. "I thought it was another of those Orson Welles things," he recalled. "But when a neighbor came pounding on our door, I found out it was Orson Yamamoto."

When the truth sank in, worries came tumbling after. Delaney knew better than anyone the sorry plight of *Yorktown*'s power plant. Six of *Yorktown*'s giant boilers were in deteriorating condition; she had steamed too far, without major refit. Under this kind of relentless pressure, the mortar between the insulating firebrick had begun to crumble. Until these boilers could be rebricked, there would be no chance that *Yorktown* could make anything approaching top speed.

Commander Delaney arrived aboard *Yorktown* just minutes ahead of Lieutenant Charles Reed Cundiff, his boiler officer. Cundiff, whose obsession with physical fitness had made him something of a celebrity, pedaled his bicycle from his home to Pier 7 in what must have been record time, even for him. He and Delaney hustled belowdecks to see about stacking new firebrick near the inefficient boilers.

At 10 P.M. buses filled with 300 recruits fresh from boot camp at Norfolk rolled up to Pier 7. In no time at all, the boots were put to work unloading provisions from three railroad freight cars that had materialized as unexpectedly as the recruits themselves. One of the boots, John Paige, from the hill country of North Carolina, worked all night and into the morning. He had twice been told to fall out of line and go below to the mess hall. Not knowing how to get below, he just went on working.

The scene at East Field, where *Yorktown's* four squadrons of planes were parked, was almost as hectic. Captain Buckmaster wanted every plane aboard by Monday morning; efforts to comply with his wishes were spurred by rumors that large formations of German bombers had been sighted off the tip of Long Island. Millard Haley and other squadron CPOs began driving their men mercilessly. Sunday night, engines started turning over at East Field, and *Yorktown's* airplanes began to taxi off the airfield and down the streets of the naval base to Pier 7, where cranes hauled them aboard.

Reason slowly returned. By December 9 rumors of German bomber fleets had been dispelled, and *Yorktown's* airplanes were unloaded and taxied back to East Field for final overhaul. *Yorktown* made a short run across the Elizabeth River to the dry dock at Portsmouth. Civilian workmen—sailors derisively called them yardbirds—swarmed aboard, and for once, the men of *Yorktown* were glad to see them.

Seaman Paige, the wide-eyed boot from North Carolina, was handed a long-handled scraper and told to help remove barnacles from *Yorktown's* hull. He had been awake for fifty-two hours, and it was too much. He began crying. "What the hell's the matter with you?" a boatswain's mate asked him. Paige explained as best he could. The boatswain's mate finally caught what he was saying: that Paige had not eaten or slept in more than two days. In a rare display of kindness the boatswain's mate took the boot to a bunk below, fetched him a three-inch-thick meat-loaf sandwich, and told him to eat and sleep. For Seaman Paige, a two-day-old war was a very long war indeed.

Wars come and go; bureaucracy goes on forever. So it was with *Yorktown*. Bureaucrats at the Navy's Bureau of Ordnance and Gunnery fired off salvos of queries and orders to Lieutenant Commander Ernest "Ernie" Davis, *Yorktown's* gunnery officer. "At one point," Davis later recalled, "they ordered me to send gun crews over to Dam Neck for training on the twenty-millimeter guns they were giving us. Hell, we already had those guns aboard and were replacing our fifty-caliber machine guns with them!"

When Davis told Washington about this, word came back to turn in the machine guns to the navy yard immediately. Davis' inclination was to comply, what with discipline and all that. But then he had another thought. "Somewhere," he recalled, "I had read that a fifty could get off six thousand rounds without a water jacket before the barrel began to curl. Twenty-four guns at six thousand rounds apiece sounded like a lot of firepower to me. Between protecting Norfolk and protecting *Yorktown*, I figured we came out first. So I kept the fifties, and I don't know if Washington ever did get its books straight on the deal."

There was so much work to be done—and little time to do it. First, of course, there was that firebrick for the faulty boilers. That would take weeks, not days, but the job was started. Then the ship had to be both replenished and lightened. Ordinarily, at full load, *Yorktown* drew 30 feet of water but to get through the Panama Canal without scraping bottom, she could not draw more than 18.5 feet. So, while ammunition and provisions were hauled aboard, oil was pumped out. That—pumping out the oil—was a problem in itself, for a carrier like *Yorktown* naturally lists seven degrees to starboard when she is low on fuel; this is caused by the weight of her stacks and superstructure, all located on the starboard side. To correct this natural list, Chief Water Tender George Vavrek had to shift the fuel that remained to portside tanks as a counterweight.

Yorktown's hull number was CV-5, because she was the fifth carrier built (after *Langley*, *Saratoga*, *Lexington*, and *Ranger*). This meant that her air squadrons—fighter, dive bomber, scout, and torpedo—were numbered VF-5, VB-5, VS-5, and VT-5 respectively. But VF-5, *Yorktown's* fighter squadron, had left the ship months earlier to participate in Army maneuvers in Louisiana, and Fighting 42 from U.S.S. *Ranger* had come aboard as a temporary replacement. The men of Fighting 42, on Sunday, December 7, had been looking forward to Fighting 5's return and to a tour ashore for themselves. It was not to be; Fighting 42 was equipped with Grumman F4F-3 Wildcats, the latest model of that stubby little airplane, and *Yorktown's* own squadron, Fighting 5, was still flying an earlier model. Because Fighting 42 was available and because it had the better aircraft, it had to go to war in a ship that was not its own.

To get to war, Fighting 42 had to scramble. Armor plate for the engines and seats of its fighters, along with new self-sealing gasoline tanks, had been lying around in East Field hangars for weeks. Now Fighting 42 had just a week to get the armor and gas tanks installed. Men from other squadrons pitched in to help, and still it was touch and go. Seaman William Federowicz, who worked until he dropped from fatigue, remembers that 700 separate screws had to be removed to install one of the new self-sealing tanks. Then all 700 screws had to be put back.

On December 16, *Yorktown* moved out of her dry dock and returned to Pier 7. As she pulled alongside, her planes were already being taxied to the dock. They all were aboard by evening, and the public-address system blared the order: "Set the special sea detail!" In compliance with the order, the officer of the deck's watch was shifted from *Yorktown's* quarterdeck to her bridge.

Sailors hauled in *Yorktown's* mooring lines, one by one, as the dock gang threw them clear. On the darkened pier the wives of the men of *Yorktown* huddled in lonely clusters. At 9:08 P.M., Captain Buckmaster ordered, "All engines back one-third!" The great carrier eased out into the stream; then wheeling slowly, she headed for the channel and the fifty-two mile run down to X-Ray Sugar, the outermost buoy of Hampton Roads.

Yorktown was on her way.

But, the men of *Yorktown* wondered, where? And for what purpose?

Great decisions, decisions an ordinary sailor could not hope to comprehend, had been in the making. One of them was the ABC-1 Staff Agreement, the "Beat Hitler First" strategy that had been hammered out even before war began; it had been ratified by President Roosevelt and Prime Minister Churchill in a secret meeting aboard the cruiser *Augusta,* when the Atlantic Charter had been signed.

The two Allied leaders had simply agreed that Hitler would have to be dealt with first, while Hirohito was to be held off as best as the circumstances might permit. Even the disaster at Pearl Harbor had not altered the basic agreement.

But something had to be done about the Japanese, lest they grab so much that there would be nothing left to defend. The response was to send *Yorktown,* three battleships, and a destroyer squadron to the Pacific at once. The battleships would presumably replace some of those destroyed or damaged at Pearl Harbor: *Arizona, California,* and *West Virginia* sunk; *Oklahoma* capsized; *Nevada* heavily damaged; *Maryland, Pennsylvania,* and *Tennessee* damaged.

In the aftermath of Pearl Harbor few people took note of the remarkable fact that none of America's three carriers in the Pacific had even been grazed. At the time of the Japanese attack, *Enterprise* was on her way to Pearl Harbor from Wake Island, where she had delivered a squadron of Marine fighters. She was due to arrive on Monday, December 8. The second carrier, *Lexington,* was on her way to Midway, delivering a Marine bomber squadron. The third,

Saratoga, was off the California coast, preparing to put into San Diego. Now *Yorktown* was on her way to join these three other warships; together, they were supposed to carry the American burden in the Pacific.

And an American burden it would surely be, for Roosevelt and Churchill were agreed that the United States would be responsible for the defense of the entire Pacific, including the British commonwealths of Australia and New Zealand.

The Japanese, too, had been making some decisions, all flowing naturally enough from their original decision to go to war. The Japanese basic war plan had been put together as early as 1938; now, with hardly a deviation (Japan's inability to innovate has often been remarked), it was being carried out.

The war had opened with three major attacks. Bombers and torpedo planes, operating from six Japanese carriers, had struck Pearl Harbor, with the intention of knocking out the U.S. Pacific fleet. The carnage had been terrible, but as has been noted, American carriers, in an extraordinary piece of luck, had escaped. Next, Japanese bombers operating out of Formosa had struck American airfields in the Philippines, easing the way for a Japanese invasion. Third, Japanese troops had stormed ashore on the Malay Peninsula.

All this was part of the Japanese fan-out strategy. With these sudden and overpowering attacks, Japan would seize the raw resources she needed to wage war. Then, having taken what she needed, she would consolidate her conquests in a great defensive perimeter stretching all the way from the Arctic to Australia.

Their initial success surprised even the Japanese. Admiral Yamamoto, the grand architect of Japanese strategy, had anticipated heavy losses in the war's opening phases.* But not a single Japanese warship had been lost in the attack on Pearl Harbor. Moreover, resistance was crumbling on the Malay Peninsula, and the Philippines seemed to offer no great difficulty.

Yet success was not at all what it seemed. Japan, in a way, had been too successful in destroying American battleships (and British, too; Japanese torpedoes and bombs had sunk *Prince of Wales* and *Repulse*). No American could any longer doubt the emergence of the carrier as the backbone of the fleet. Thus, in American yards new carriers were laid down, and battleship construction was cut back. The day when the gap would be closed moved closer.

Japanese planes would have done more at Pearl Harbor had they destroyed the immense oil tanks that fueled the U.S. fleet, the docks that maintained it, and the shops that repaired it. All these facilities remained relatively unscathed, and Japan was to pay dearly for it.

There was, too, the *way* in which Japan chose to open hostilities—striking without a formal declaration of war while its diplomats still talked peace. Americans became aroused; the will to fight built up overnight. It might have been otherwise.

Japan's war hawks could not comprehend this kind of thinking. All they could see was victory after victory, all

---

* The admiral, however, was a realist. He had estimated that Japan would run up successes in the first six months and that thereafter American industrial superiority would begin to assert itself. "I must tell you," he said to Prince Fuminaro Konoye in 1940, "that should the war be prolonged for two or three years, I have no confidence in our ultimate victory." Yamamoto was killed in April, 1943, when his plane was shot down by American P-38 fighters.

without serious cost. They saw no reason to consolidate their success; they did see good reason to quicken their effort. Thus, they decided to move against three more targets—Port Moresby on the Papua Peninsula of New Guinea and the island of Tulagi in the Solomons, to gain mastery of the air over the Coral Sea; Midway Atoll and the western Aleutian Islands, to expand the outer perimeter and to challenge the U.S. fleet to a decisive engagement; and New Caledonia, Fiji, and Samoa, to isolate Australia from the United States.*

The Battle of the Coral Sea, *Yorktown's* first major encounter, was fought to deny the Coral Sea to Japan. Midway, *Yorktown's* second (and final) battle, was America's reply to the Japanese challenge. And there never was an invasion of New Caledonia, Fiji, or Samoa because America won at Midway.

Such, then, were the decisions that would shape *Yorktown's* future. As *Yorktown* steamed out of Norfolk on December 16, 1941, no man aboard could discern even the outlines of these mighty forces that would soon roll over the carrier.

* Much of the basic strategy is discussed by Samuel Eliot Morison in his *History of United States Naval Operations in World War II*. But as we shall see, he is not always reliable on operational details.

Chapter Two

★ ★ ★ ★ ★ ★ ★

★ ★ ★ On the morning of December 17, *Yorktown*, off Cape Hatteras, was as crowded as a cattle boat. In addition to her own airplanes, she carried Consolidated PBY Catalina amphibious airplanes for delivery to the Canal Zone defense force. And besides her own crew, she carried hundreds of extras to be dropped off as reinforcements for Navy patrol squadrons at Panama.

She also carried a number of stowaways. The Navy counts noses daily, and a few minutes before 8 A.M. on the seventeenth, all hands not actually on watch lined up for muster, for a nose count that no one expected to produce any surprises. But when muster was finished, *Yorktown's* master-at-arms approached Commander Jocko Clark, the executive officer. Lieutenant Bill Crenshaw, *Yorktown's* main engines officer, was nearby and witnessed the exchange. "There's something wrong here," the master-at-arms said. "We got thirty more men aboard than we oughta. They're wandering around the hangar deck like a bunch of orphans."

"Get them up here!" Clark ordered.

The frightened sailors appeared one by one, lining up in

ranks for the commander's inspection. Clark hobbled up and down in front of them on his game leg. It had been injured and reinjured in airplane crashes, but nothing the medics recommended could force him into retirement. He pushed his chin into a sailor's face. "Who told you to come aboard this ship?" he asked.

"You did, sir," the sailor replied.

The same question brought the same reply as Clark went down the line.

It was nothing less than the truth. The stowaway sailors were boots who had wandered down to Pier 7 from the recruit camp to watch *Yorktown*'s departure. Whenever Commander Clark had spotted one, he had roared, "Don't just stand there! Get aboard and lend 'em a hand." They all had done just that, and once aboard, they had been too frightened to ask about getting off. On the trip to the Canal they slept on top of hangar deck cargo.

The five-day run from Norfolk to Colón was a time to get ready, and *Yorktown* needed every minute she could find.

The ship's two best welders, Norris Hook and Paul Vander, were ordered by Chief Shipfitter Joe Kisela to work on the new 20-millimeter gun mounts. The welders crawled up on scaffolds, teetering high above the sea, to anchor the new guns. No sooner were they installed than the Marines from *Yorktown*'s 5th Division, who had been assigned to the old .50-caliber machine guns, were taught to fire them. Like any good warship skipper, Captain Buckmaster had only one policy on ammunition—shoot it.

Yorktown had eight 5-inch guns, mounted in pairs just below her flight deck, at each of its four corners. These, *Yorktown*'s biggest guns, were manned by sailors from ship's company. For practice, the sailors would fire a round from the big guns, and the Marines would use this shell-burst as a target for their 20-millimeter guns.

In addition, *Yorktown* had four quadruple sets of 1.1-inch machine guns, two forward and two aft of her super-structure. Lieutenant Commander Ernie Davis, the gun-nery officer, despised them as Rube Goldbergs. They were the same gun mounts that the British called Chicago Pianos. They jammed constantly and rarely gave more than two or three seconds' worth of uninterrupted fire. The only way they could be fired was to place a gunner's mate under each mount, flat on his back, armed with wrenches and ham-mers. From that position, he could correct the jamming.

It was on the way to Panama, too, that Radioman Alvis "Speedy" Attaway began installing a secret weapon on *Yorktown's* highest yardarm. It was called IFF, for iden-tification, friend or foe, and it was supposed to emit a spe-cial electronic signal that would be answered by *York-town's* airplanes. In this way, *Yorktown's* planes would not be shot at by their own ship when they returned from mis-sions.

There were other improvements. In Fighting 42, ord-nancemen replaced the old telescopic gunsights in the Wildcat fighters with more modern electric gunsights. Training in Bombing 5, always unusually intensive, tight-ened up even more. "Every man had to learn every-one else's job," Seaman Harry "Dutch" Schanbacher re-called later. Among Bombing 5's officers was Lieutenant Sam Adams, a pioneer in developing the Navy's steep-dive bombing tactics. Before Adams and a few others had set to work, Navy pilots had been trained to spiral slowly toward their targets.

To the men of *Yorktown*, the ship was personified by Commander Clark. He was everywhere in those first days at sea, passing wrenches to mechanics, pushing planes across the deck. His gimpy leg was testament to his long service as a carrier pilot. Junior officers often feared Clark, but the white-hatted enlisted men loved him. "Let's go to Tokyo!" he roared. His enthusiasm was infectious.

Prior to arrival at Colón, *Yorktown* was again disguised, this time as *Enterprise*. The ship's lettering was changed, and the numbering, CV-5, was changed to CV-6. Passengers scheduled to debark at Panama were cautioned to keep *Yorktown*'s secret. As final insurance, Captain Buckmaster passed word that no one would get liberty.

Then, as Captain Buckmaster, impeccable in his dress whites, strode down *Yorktown*'s gangway to make his official courtesy calls at Colón, the boatswain's mate of the watch stepped into a small cubbyhole off the quarterdeck which housed a microphone for the ship's public-address system and a ship's bell. From force of habit—he had done the same thing a hundred times before—he rang the bell four times, one clang for each of the skipper's stripes. Automatically he bellowed into the microphone, "*Yorktown*, departing! *Yorktown*, departing!" This meant, in Navy jargon, that the captain was departing. The boatswain's mate's voice, amplified a dozen times, reverberated along Colón's waterfront and down its narrow alleys.

Japanese agents, who had probably already guessed *Yorktown*'s real identity, now knew it for certain. And

Buckmaster, the secret out, granted liberty to a fourth of *Yorktown*'s crew. For those lucky enough to get ashore, to Colón's celebrated Cocoanut Grove district, it was a night to remember and to savor years later in stag retellings. Seaman George Weise, who did not make liberty that night, later remembered that some Yorktowners "were so bent out of shape that they had to be swung aboard in cargo nets. The only time I ever saw anything like it was years later, in the movie *Mister Roberts*."

Yorktown cleared the Canal in eleven hours. She was hardly through it on December 22 when the destroyer *Walke*, patrolling off her port bow, reported an underwater sound contact. *Yorktown* manned battle stations as *Walke* and two other destroyers fired depth charges. With the emotions of the time, everyone was sure that a Japanese submarine had been sunk; more likely, a large whale had been disturbed. Postwar records indicate that the Japanese had nine submarines in the eastern Pacific at that precise moment, and all were somewhere between San Pedro, California, and Vancouver, British Columbia. They were primed to shell West Coast cities on Christmas morning. But that order was canceled at the last moment when spies in Panama reported that *Yorktown* had passed through the Canal and was loose in the Pacific.

Yorktown cleared the Panamanian coast, bending on twenty-seven knots, the best she could do until her boilers were in top shape, and headed north for San Diego. The dash for San Diego demonstrated the value of radar, for Radioman Speedy Attaway's readings permitted *Yorktown* to cruise at best speed in darkness, confident that she was well clear of the coastline.

Having cleared the Atlantic and entered the Pacific, the war—to the men of *Yorktown*—suddenly seemed closer. Their egos, never entirely restrained, grew, even as heroic Marine defenders surrendered on Wake Island, as Hong Kong fell, as the Japanese pedaled down the Malay Peninsula on their foldaway bicycles. Rear Admiral Chester Nimitz replaced the unfortunate Admiral Husband Kimmel as Pacific fleet commander. And the transport *Connecticut* was sunk by a Japanese submarine in the mouth of the Colombia River.

Commander Clark, circulating among Yorktowners, heard caustic comments about Pearl Harbor, comments like "They sure must have been dopin' off out there" and "They probably were all sacked out at the New Senator or one of them other houses."

Clark did not like this kind of talk. On December 29, one day out of San Diego, he published this memo:

To All Hands
From the Executive Officer:
Due to the dastardly action of the Japanese, our Navy suffered a serious reverse in the Hawaiian area on December 7, 1941. There will be much discussion about this in the months to come, and particularly if we should come in contact with those of the Navy who were present on that occasion.

All personnel of this vessel are enjoined to avoid any semblance of criticism of any of our naval units then present in the Hawaii sector, or of the personnel attached. It must be presumed that those who were on the spot did the best they could under the circumstances, and that no one should be blamed for what happened.

The events of that fateful day are past, water under the

bridge, so to speak; and the future will bring ample opportunity for us to even the score. There is too much work
ahead of us to indulge in fruitless or needless criticism.

Rather, we should adopt the role of the listener, and
offer comfort and sympathy to those who have suffered. We
should ever look forward with grim determination to the
time when we will wrest from the enemy the temporary
advantage he has obtained through his treachery, and we
should concentrate our efforts and actions toward the
righteous victory that will ultimately be ours.

The message had a salubrious effect; for the time being
at least, it silenced some of the big talk.

When *Yorktown* arrived at San Diego on December 30,
some of her planes were ordered ashore to the North Island
naval air station, to be available to defend the port against
a rumored enemy air attack.

Yorktown remained at San Diego for seven frantic days.
It was during this layover that she received the extra aircraft she would need in the weeks to come for replacement
of the planes she would lose in combat. Getting these
spares stowed was the responsibility of Lieutenant A. C.
"Ace" Emerson, *Yorktown*'s hangar officer, and his strong
right arm, Everett "Robbie" Robinson, boatswain's mate.

It was the men who made *Yorktown* what she was. Topside, it was Jocko Clark. Down in the hangar deck, it was
Robinson. He had a voice like a bullhorn and muscles like
a wrestler. The men of *Yorktown* called him the Bull-
dog. The hangar deck was his domain, and no man entered his kingdom with irreverence—no man, no officer.

Robinson's family lived in San Diego, and he had not
seen them in fourteen months. But getting his ship ready
for war came first. Every night his boss, Lieutenant Com-

mander Murr Arnold, had to push him—almost literally
—down the gangway. He never left *Yorktown* until 9:30
at night, and he was back with her every morning by dawn.

Robinson and his crew hauled 42 spare aircraft aboard
and strapped them—like light bulbs—to the ceiling of
the hangar deck. Wings and other spare parts were stacked
along the bulkheads. The 42 additional craft gave *Yorktown* 129 airplanes, more than any other carrier in the U.S.
Navy.

On New Year's Eve, Rear Admiral Frank Jack Fletcher
came up *Yorktown's* gangway with his personal staff. *Yorktown* was to be his flagship for newly formed Task Force
17. Fletcher was leather-tough and spare; his face was
creased from a thousand nights and days on the bridges of
warships. Sailors were to call him Black Jack Fletcher, although his hair was blond and his eyes were blue. It was
to be Black Jack Fletcher who would take *Yorktown* and
the ships accompanying her into the battles of the Coral
Sea and Midway.

Two other veterans joined *Yorktown* at San Diego. One
was Chief Carpenter's Mate Thomas Coleman. He had
been piped over the side into retirement in mid-1941 and
had actually bought a chicken ranch. When war came, he
wanted to go back—and to *Yorktown*. With more than
thirty years of service, he had no trouble pulling the right
strings to get orders assigning him to his old ship. He was
waiting for her at dockside when she pulled in.

The second old-timer to come aboard was Chief Quartermaster Henry Peltier, who had seen service in World
War I. He had reenlisted on December 8, fully expecting
to be assigned to a garbage scow in San Diego harbor. Post-

ing to *Yorktown* and to Fletcher's staff was an exhilarating bonus. His first assignment was to inventory all charts and all sailing directions, documents vital to sea navigation. "Complete," Peltier told Commander Gerard Galpin, Fletcher's operations officer, "except for the South Pacific."

"Great Scott," said the commander, "that's where we're going!" He promptly ordered Peltier ashore to requisition the missing materials.

Yorktown's destination, naturally enough, was supposed to be a closely guarded secret. But the word—Samoa— soon made the rounds. Lieutenant Commander Murr Arnold told Captain Buckmaster that he was surprised *Yorktown* was going to Samoa. "I was positive," he told the skipper, "we'd be heading for Pearl."

"Where did you hear it was Samoa?" the captain demanded.

"I didn't hear it," Arnold replied. "I saw it. On the beach. There's a stack of crates down at Broadway Pier marked 'Samoa—Via *Yorktown.*' "

Yorktown was indeed bound for Samoa. She put to sea at 1:17 P.M. on January 6, escorting the 7th Marine Regiment loaded aboard the Matson excursion liners *Monterey*, *Matsonia*, and *Lurline*. Accompanying the liners were the ammunition ship *Lassen*, the Navy tanker *Kaskaskia*, the repair ship *Jupiter*, four destroyers that had traveled with *Yorktown* from the Atlantic—*Sims*, *Walke*, *Russell*, and *Hughes*—and two light cruisers, *St. Louis* and *Louisville*.

Yorktown lost her first plane on January 7, when Ensign Edward "Ed" Bassett's Wildcat splashed after takeoff. Ensign William "Bill" Woollen made it two in a row the next day, and Ensign Walter "Walt" Haas lost a third fighter on January 12. All three pilots were recovered, but the planes were gone forever, and some of *Yorktown*'s officers began to wonder if there might be something seriously amiss with the aircraft. Fears rose on January 14, when Ensign Richard "Dick" Wright lost a fourth Wildcat. Lieutenant Commander Oscar Pederson, skipper of Fighting 42, ordered his mechanics to tear a Wildcat apart, if necessary, to find out what the trouble was. It would be months before the answer was found.

On January 11, *Yorktown*'s radio received news that a Japanese submarine was shelling Pago Pago, Samoa, *Yorktown*'s destination. Other Japanese submarines were reported operating south of Hawaii; these were the same submarines that had been stationed off the California coast for the Christmas shelling that had never occurred. They were now heading back to their advance base at Kwajalein, in the Marshall Islands.

That same evening *Yorktown*'s radio picked up worse news. The carrier *Saratoga* had been torpedoed about 350 miles southwest of Pearl Harbor and was limping toward Bremerton for extensive repairs. That meant that the operational carrier force in the Pacific was now right back to where it had been when *Yorktown* had emerged from the Canal—three ships.

The men of *Yorktown* were further sobered the night of January 12, when Seaman William Reckhouse fell overboard. One sailor saw the accident and threw a cork life ring over the side. "I saw Reckhouse swim toward the ring," Seaman Ed Cavanaugh later recalled. "He was about ten feet from it when he went down." There was nothing anyone could do. *Yorktown* represented one-third of America's carrier strength in the Pacific, and she had the three Matson liners loaded with Marines to think about. The task force steamed on. "It was the saddest moment of my life," recalled Ensign John Lorenz. "This big ship with over two thousand men, and we couldn't help just one man."

On Sunday, January 18, memorial services for Reckhouse were conducted by Lieutenant Commander Frank Hamilton, *Yorktown*'s chaplain. That same day, the repair ship *Jupiter*, her condensers collapsing under the pace *Yorktown* was setting, signaled that she could make no more than six knots. *Yorktown* pushed ahead, and little *Jupiter* dropped out of sight.

As *Yorktown* approached Samoa, Admiral Fletcher decided that the submarine danger was minimal. The I-boat that had shelled Pago Pago, he reasoned, would not have surfaced and revealed herself if she had not been at the tag end of her patrol. Surely, by now, she would be hundreds of miles away. On the night of January 19, Fletcher ordered the transports to run into Pago Pago, while *Yorktown*, the cruisers, and the destroyers stood off-shore in a defensive crescent.

To the north, over the horizon, was another task force, centered on *Yorktown*'s sister ship, *Enterprise*, under the command of Rear Admiral William F. Halsey. On January 23, with the Marines safely ashore and new orders in hand, *Yorktown* and *Enterprise*, just barely visible to each other, headed northwest with their consorts.

Other forces were also on the move. Vice Admiral Chuichi Nagumo, who had commanded the strike against Pearl Harbor, was steaming from Truk Island, in the Carolines, toward the Indian Ocean. He delayed long enough en route to deliver a devastating sideswipe at Rabaul, the strategic port on New Britain Island, north of New Guinea. The attack was so fierce that a follow-up invasion encountered little more than token opposition.

American forces in the Philippines were withdrawing into Bataan and the island of Corregidor. On January 25 the Japanese submarine *I-73* boldly shelled Midway Atoll.

It was a time when the Japanese could do no wrong. Many Americans—not all of them civilians—began to talk of Japanese invincibility. And it was at this dramatic moment that *Yorktown* received new orders from Pearl Harbor. Captain Buckmaster passed the word to a cheering crew. *Yorktown* was going on the offensive, to smash Japanese bases in the Gilbert Islands.

Chapter Three

★ ★ ★ ★ ★ ★ ★

★ ★ ★ *Yorktown* was ordered to strike three Japanese outposts—Makin, Mili, and Jaluit. Admiral Halsey, with *Enterprise,* was ordered farther north, to attack three more bases in the Marshall Islands. It was not much; but it was something, and it might be enough to force the Japanese to disperse their forces to defend against these irritating American hit-and-run tactics. That, at least, was the hopeful thinking of American planners.

Enterprise parted company with *Yorktown* on January 28; she had twice as far to go. While waiting for *Enterprise* to get into position, *Yorktown* tried to deceive the enemy. Nights, she and her screen would dart toward the Gilberts; before dawn, they would reverse course and steam slowly toward the point from which they had started. Fletcher knew that long-range Japanese flying boats, lacking radar, could spot him only during daylight hours. If they did see him, he wanted them to report he was heading away from the Gilberts, not toward them.

At dusk on January 30 the game ended, and *Yorktown* raced for the point from which she was to launch her strike. That evening Fletcher summoned his aerologist to

Flag Plot, in *Yorktown*'s superstructure. The aerologist was Lieutenant Commander Hubert "Hubie" Strange, who had studied meteorology at Cal Tech after his graduation from Annapolis.

"What's it going to be like in the morning?" Fletcher asked.

"A lot like now, Admiral," Strange replied. "Sloppy. This mass of frontal weather will stay with the ship, going in and coming out. The air group probably will have foul weather all the way into the targets. And back, too."

Fletcher decided to attack anyway. The plan called for simultaneous strikes by both *Yorktown* and *Enterprise*. That way, Fletcher reasoned, enemy defense forces would be fragmented. Strange was dismissed, with orders to bring his final weather data to the bridge at 4 A.M.

Not long after dark, Ernie Davis, the gunnery officer, sent Ensign John Lorenz to check the ready ammunition lockers for the five-inch guns. He wanted to make sure that they were secure against foul weather. What he could not do, however, was guarantee that the shells would fire properly. Davis had received a secret dispatch from the Bureau of Ordnance and Gunnery listing the lot numbers of defective five-inch ammunition. Some of this defective ammunition had been fired at Pearl Harbor; it had exploded prematurely over Honolulu, and its shrapnel had killed a number of civilians, for which the Japanese were originally blamed. *Yorktown*'s five-inch ammunition came from other lots of that same defective shipment.

Yorktown started launching her planes before dawn, sending forty-two pilots into weather worse than anything any of them had ever seen in the Atlantic. Each dive bomber carried a single 500-pound bomb; each torpedo bomber carried three 500-pound bombs.

First off was a twenty-eight-plane strike against Jaluit, presumed to be the most important target. Lieutenant Commander Bob Armstrong led the seventeen SBD Dauntless dive bombers; Lieutenant Commander Joe Taylor led the eleven TBD Devastator torpedo planes. A second force, nine dive bombers under Lieutenant Commander Bill Burch, was sent against Makin, and Lieutenant Wally Short took five dive bombers to Mili. All fighter planes remained aboard, to protect *Yorktown* against a possible attack.

Intermittent thunderstorms made footing hazardous on the flight deck, and sometimes visibility dropped to fifty yards. Electrician's Mate John Metcalf of Bombing 5 noticed a flash and glow high in the sky ahead of *Yorktown;* it was not until later that he realized what it was.

The major strike, against Jaluit (onetime capital of the Marshalls), was under the overall command of Commander Curtis Smiley. Most of Smiley's planes, slammed around by the horrendous weather, arrived over the target alone. They managed to find a few holes in the overcast and pounced through them to the targets below.

Hits were made on a seaplane tender and a cargo ship; near-misses, on a third vessel. After dropping their bombs, the pilots swung back to strafe with their forward-firing .50-calibers, then pulled up sharply to allow their rear gunners a go with .30-calibers. Not all the Jaluit-bound planes got to drop their bombs; some never found the atoll. They had to jettison their bombs and streak for home. Ensign Tom Ellison's TBD had only two gallons of fuel left when he came aboard *Yorktown*.

The attack no doubt excited the Japanese below. Up above Jaluit it was confusing enough. Because of the bad weather, the American planes had trouble finding one another. Ensign Ben Preston of Bombing 5 had so many near collisions that his rear gunner, Harry Cowden, finally offered a bit of advice. "What do you say, Mister Preston, we get out of here and go fight the Japs?" he shouted in the intercom.

At Makin, Commander Burch's planes cracked open, but failed to sink an 8,000-ton seaplane tender. They did manage to sink two large flying boats moored in the lagoon. At Mili, Lieutenant Short's planes, failing to sight any floating targets, unloaded on what they hoped was a military warehouse and ammunition dump.

Yorktown's bullhorn was hooked into the tactical radio frequency being used by her aircraft so that the flight- and hangar-deck crews could get a blow-by-blow account of the attacks. At 8:11 A.M. a voice crackled over the speakers. The news was not good.

"This is five-T-seven," the voice said. "Five-T-seven and five-T-six are landing alongside one of the northwest islands of Jaluit. That is all." The men of Torpedo 5 knew that 5-T-7 belonged to their executive officer, Lieutenant H. T. "Dub" Johnson; five-T-six was Ensign Herbert Hein's plane. Years later, after his rescue from a Japanese prisoner-of-war camp in 1945, Hein told what had happened.

They had dropped their bombs and were heading back

for *Yorktown;* Johnson was leading. Then, with no sun visible to give him an obvious correction, Johnson made a mistake not uncommon to mariners: he misread his compass by 180 degrees. Instead of heading east, he headed west, and he and Hein, following behind, continued on that course for twenty minutes. When Johnson realized what he had done, he turned around, passed over Jaluit again, but quickly realized he did not have enough gasoline to get home. He and Hein dumped their bombsights overboard; Johnson sent his radio message to *Yorktown,* and the two planes ditched in the sea.

Each TBD carried a crew of three. None of the six men aboard the two planes was hurt when they ditched. They inflated two life rafts and paddled to Gebu, an island at the extreme northwestern corner of Jaluit Atoll. There they found a small village and friendly Micronesians. Two days later the Japanese landed fifty men on the island while a four-engine seaplane sat down in the lagoon to seal their escape route toward the sea. All six men surrendered.

At 8:12 A.M., *Yorktown* began recovering her aircraft. When all who were coming home were home, she turned east and began churning up speed to escape pursuit. As the big warship moaned and rumbled from the high-speed vibrations, Captain Buckmaster began totting up the strike's cost.

It was then that everyone realized the significance of the flash in the sky that Electrician's Mate Metcalf had seen. It had been the collision of two TBDs; they had struck each other minutes after takeoff. Neither plane was ever sighted; all men aboard were lost. The two planes that ditched off Gebu pushed the count up to four. Two other

SBDs had collided over Jaluit; that made it six. A seventh plane, an SBD piloted by Ensign T. A. Reeves, went down returning to *Yorktown*, but a destroyer picked up Reeves and his gunner, Seaman Lonnie Gooch.

Seven aircraft lost, sixteen men gone, and none of this damage caused by the enemy. Against that was the destruction *Yorktown*'s airmen had reported. But as usual with young men in their first brush with war, the reports had been hopelessly exaggerated. Intelligence reports, months later, confirmed that Japan had little of military importance in the Gilberts except a few seaplanes.

Farther north, although they had clear weather and better targets, Halsey and *Enterprise* had done no better. *Enterprise*'s planes made the mistake of rendezvousing within sight of the enemy before attacking. This gave a nest of Japanese submarines anchored at Kwajalein time to "pull the plug" and settle safely to the bottom of the lagoon; it also gave defending Zeros time to get into the air. Four of *Enterprise*'s planes were shot down, and the war's first kamikaze very nearly crashed into *Enterprise*'s flight deck. One of the accompanying cruisers took a bomb hit.

Such was the uninspiring record of America's first naval offensive in the Pacific.* But the men aboard *Yorktown* were elated; after all, they had done something, and they thought they had done a lot more. When the news was published in the States, a similar kind of euphoria resulted. "Haul Out With Halsey!" became a catchphrase in the newspapers. *Yorktown* men, noticing that not

---

* *Lexington* should have had the honor. She had headed for Wake Island to blast the Japanese who had seized that outpost from the Marines. But on January 23 her accompanying tanker was torpedoed. Her refueling source lost, *Lexington* turned around and came home to Pearl Harbor.

much was being said about them, soon had an earthy para-
phrase of their own.

Still steaming eastward, *Yorktown* picked up a bogey
on her radar screen at 11:17 A.M. General quarters was
sounded, and Lieutenant Vince McCormack of Fighting
42 was dispatched (vectored, in Navy jargon) to hunt it
down, but the snooper got away. At 1:07 P.M., *Yorktown*'s
cranky radar picked up another bogey; this one was dead
ahead, thirty-two miles away. General quarters was again
sounded, and in minutes an awesome collection of artillery
was manned.

Four of *Yorktown*'s twenty-four new 20-millimeter guns
had been mounted on the flight deck in a flat space
formerly occupied by a nest of boats. The other twenty
guns were divided into groups of five, one near every pair
of 5-inch guns. Strung out along *Yorktown*'s catwalks and
at her bow and stern were the .50-caliber machine guns
Ernie Davis had refused to turn in at Norfolk. Davis also
had somehow come up with more than fifty .30-caliber
machine guns. Volunteers grabbed them and made a surprising discovery. The .30-caliber rested in a fork mount
which had a hollow handle. The posts supporting *Yorktown*'s catwalk lifelines were also hollow. The volunteers
discovered that a broom or swab handle, sawed to the right
length, fitted into the lifeline post and the gun handle.
With a minimum of equipment, any sailor could go into
the machine gun business. Dozens of them did just that.
Yorktown bristled with more guns than a Mexican rev-
olution movie.

Ensigns Scott "Scotty" McCuskey and John Adams were
sent aloft to hunt down the new intruder. They had hardly

taken off when the bogey pulled into clear sight of the men aboard *Yorktown*. She was an immense, waddling Kawanishi flying boat, nicknamed Mavis, and she was heading straight for *Yorktown*. When the big flying boat was still about ten miles away, Captain Buckmaster put *Yorktown* into a hard right turn; the big ship heeled over like a motorboat rounding a buoy.

Lieutenant Oxy Hurlbert was in Sky Control, a tiny, unprotected platform just above *Yorktown*'s bridge. Below Hurlbert, on a slightly larger platform, was Ernie Davis. From these exposed points, the two men directed *Yorktown*'s gunnery.

Hurlbert and Davis watched in fascination as the Japanese flying boat ducked into a cloud, McCuskey and Adams in hot pursuit. Others who were tuned in to the pilots' radio frequency reported that the two ensigns were yelling like cowboys. The flying boat never came out of the cloud. Just its wreckage—chunks of wing and flaming bits of fuselage—came tumbling down.

"Burn, you son of a bitch, burn!" Jocko Clark shouted. The crew cheered. Another cheer went up when all hands on the flight and hangar decks heard Scotty McCuskey's cry, amplified through loudspeakers, "We just shot his ass off!"

Seconds after the remains of the flying boat dropped into the ocean, a tremendous underwater explosion rocked *Yorktown*. It was, presumably, the plane's bombs exploding. Machinist's Mate Worth Hare, stationed in *Yorktown*'s after engine room, later recalled the explosion vividly: "For the first time, I felt I was at war."

Commander Delaney, the chief engineer, also stationed

in the bowels of *Yorktown,* called the smoke watch to ask what was going on. The watch was a lone sailor stationed high in *Yorktown's* island; it was his job to compare the color of the smoke coming from *Yorktown's* triple stack against a chart. By the color of the smoke, *Yorktown's* engineers could judge the efficiency of the boilers. The smoke watch also acted as the battle eyes for the men sweating it out below. When Delaney asked what was going on, the excited sailor replied, "Those must have been his bombs or depth charges, Mister Delaney. They just shot his ass off!"

Weeks earlier, Fighting 42's maintenance men had prepared a special award for the first pilot who shot down a Japanese plane. The prize was a multicolored jacket emblazoned with dozens of strange and curious decorations and a hat that looked something like a fez. When Mc-Cuskey and Adams landed, the maintenance crews swarmed around them. The award was divided: one of the victors got the jacket; the other got the hat.

Shortly before 11 A.M. on February 6, *Yorktown* came steaming up the narrow channel to Pearl Harbor. It was the first time *Yorktown* had put into the great base in ten months, and her men simply could not believe what they saw. That day Dutch Schanbacher summed up the feelings of most Yorktowners in his diary:

> So this is Pearl Harbor, bastion of the Pacific. My God, this is a regular graveyard for ships! *Nevada* is sticking in the mud of the channel. *West Virginia's* cage mast is sticking out at a crazy angle. Only *Arizona's* main deck is visible. *Utah* is on her side, and other hulls are spread around. Fuel oil from sunken ships is so thick on the water that boats

don't even make a wake. Fumes are everywhere. No smoking is allowed on Ford Island except in the club and the coffee shop. Buildings have no roofs. Hangars are a sorry mess. Aircraft hulls are burnt to a crisp, and machinery in the shops is so much rubble.

Captain Buckmaster must have been especially moved. One year earlier, before he had taken command of *Yorktown*, he had been commanding officer of Ford Island naval air station. Little was left of his old command.

Yorktown made a graceful full turn around Ford Island before she moved to her berth. As she circled, other vessels cheered ship, an old British custom almost unknown in the U.S. Navy. As she passed, Yorktowners could hear the salutes: "Hip, hip," from a single voice, and then a mighty "Hooray!"

Realists aboard *Yorktown* may have wondered just what they had done to deserve such a tribute. But it was not so much for what *Yorktown* had done; the salute was for the fact that she was there. *Yorktown*, as every sailor knew, was East Coast, and her arrival at Pearl Harbor meant that reinforcements were beginning to come through.

In her ten days at Pearl Harbor, *Yorktown* replaced her stock of defective five-inch ammunition, loaded up on provisions, and took aboard more spare aircraft parts. And Fighting 42's mechanics continued their investigation of those troublesome Wildcats.

Jocko Clark was promoted to captain and transferred out of the ship he had done so much for. The new executive officer was Commander Dixie Kiefer. No one thought that *Yorktown* would be lucky enough to get two outstanding executive officers in a row, but Kiefer relieved many doubts in his first official order: he granted liberty to all hands, "commencing immediately."

On February 14, Honolulu newspapers recounted for the first time the story of the Marshalls-Gilberts raid. That night, *Yorktown's* men were the toast of Oahu. It was free drinks all around.

At 10:49 A.M. on February 16, *Yorktown* was under way. By midnight she was well below Oahu, heading southwest. Escorting her were the same four destroyers that had accompanied her through the Canal, along with the cruisers *Louisville* and *St. Louis*. She was joined by two more destroyers, *Anderson* and *Hammann*. One day *Hammann* was to die at her side.

While *Yorktown* and her escorts ran south of Oahu, her sister carriers were also busy. *Lexington,* on February 20, hit Rabaul. The raid should have worked, for all of Japan's carriers were then in the Indian Ocean or in their home ports. Unfortunately, a snooper detected *Lexington* when she was still far at sea. Bombers came out to meet her from New Britain, and the best *Lexington* could do was to put up a brilliant defensive battle. Lieutenant Edward "Butch" O'Hare distinguished himself by shooting down five Japanese bombers in six minutes that day. Four days later, on February 24, *Enterprise's* airplanes struck Wake Island while her escorting cruisers and destroyers bombarded Japanese positions.

Yorktown's assignment was less exciting. She cruised back and forth south of the Equator, protecting the lifeline to Australia. The news she picked up by radio was all bad. Singapore had fallen. The Japanese had parachuted into Sumatra and had invaded Bali, Borneo, and Java. The Allied naval force defending Java had been madly mauled; five Allied cruisers and five destroyers had gone down in two days of battle.

On March 6, *Lexington* eased over the eastern horizon, accompanied by four cruisers and eight destroyers. "Our force filled the sea from horizon to horizon. Everywhere you looked there were ships. It made us feel real good," reported Seaman Tom Edwards, who observed the awesome sight from his Gun 7 position. He also remembers the birth of the *Yorktown* remark "Haul ass with Halsey—but fight with Fletch!" It was the *Yorktown* crew's sardonic reply to *Enterprise's* getting all the headlines.

Command centers in both carriers received orders from Admiral Nimitz to make a strike against Rabaul and Gasmata, Japanese bases on New Britain Island, to shield the movement of Allied troops into New Caledonia. But the orders were hurriedly canceled. The Japanese were making their move, shelling Lae and Salamaua, on the northern coast of New Guinea, after which their troops stormed ashore.

Lae and Salamaua were across the rugged Owen Stanley Mountains from the great Allied base of Port Moresby, sole remaining foothold north of Australia. Port Moresby had to be held.

Thus far, Japan had pushed her troops ashore in Malaya, the Philippines, Java, Sumatra, and the Celebes without interference. Now, U.S. strategists reasoned, perhaps the enemy ships and men could be caught on the New Guinea beaches and wiped out. The plan was to hit them with the few Army Air Corps B-17s available in Australia and the more than 100 airplanes from *Yorktown* and *Lexington*.

By March 10 the two U.S. carriers had moved into the Gulf of Papua, along the southern coast of New Guinea. They dared not sail around the edge of the Papua Peninsula, into the Bismarck Sea, for that would have put them within easy range of the great Japanese base at Rabaul, on the island of New Britain.

There was only one way to get at the Japanese—fly over the Stanleys and down the mountains to the beaches. Planners of the attack had discovered a pass through the mountains only 7,500 feet high, as against the usual mountain elevation of 15,000 feet. But 7,500 feet was bad enough. Pilots of the torpedo bombers were particularly worried: Could their sluggish TBDs, lugging 1,000 pounds of bombs, work their way up to that altitude?

At 7:11 A.M. on March 10, *Yorktown* put up a protective umbrella of six Wildcat fighters, accompanied by four Dauntless dive bombers carrying depth charges for anti-submarine defenses. By 8:15 the first section of the strike force—thirteen SBDs under Lieutenant Commander Bill Burch and twelve TBDs under Lieutenant Commander Joe Taylor—was away. Following close behind was Lieutenant Commander Bob Armstrong with seventeen more SBDs. Lieutenant Commander Oscar Pederson, leading ten Wildcats as cover, caught up with them later, and the slow climb over the Stanleys began.

Each SBD carried one 500-pound bomb and two 100-pound bombs. The TBDs carried two 500-pound bombs.

By 10 A.M. they all were making their ascent. At 10:15 lookouts aboard *Yorktown* had spotted eighteen U.S. Army B-17s overhead at 16,000 feet, heading northeast to coordinate their attack with that of the carrier planes.

The 104 planes from the two carriers were guided to the 7,500-foot pass by Lieutenant Commander William Ault of *Lexington,* who circled above the gap to provide a radio beacon. The TBDs, to the surprise of their pilots and crews, made it up the mountains and through the pass. Radioman Bob Egger, rear gunner for pilot Sid Quick, reported that on the way up they got an unexpected, but welcome, lift from updrafts.

The attack was a fiasco. By the time the Americans arrived, most of the Japanese transports had departed. The skippers of these ships had taken part in invasions before and had learned how to get in and out fast. The final score for the 122 planes (including the high-flying B17s, a type which never was able to hit a ship 16,000 feet below) was one large transport, one large minesweeper, and an ancient light cruiser that had been converted into a repair ship.

By noon all of *Yorktown*'s planes were safely home. *Lexington* had lost one plane. The pilots were again convinced that they had hit the Japanese hard. By their own inflated estimates, they had destroyed three cargo ships at Lae and six at Salamaua.

All were to agree, however, that their equipment needed a lot of improvement. Dive bomber pilots complained that their telescopic bombsights tended to fog up from condensation during dives from high altitude. Just as bad, many of their electrical bomb releases failed to work. A number of the pilots were forced to lean out of the cockpit, line up the target by seaman's eye, and then yank on the manual bomb release.

In at least one SBD an altimeter jammed so that the radioman erroneously advised his pilot to release his bombload when the plane was still two miles above the target. Most radios were inoperative, apparently victims of tropical humidity.

One might have wondered when things would begin to go right for the U.S. Navy. But these young men were full of spirit, ready to make the best of anything. They were sure that they had given the Japanese a pasting.

Chapter Four

★ ★ ★ ★ ★ ★ ★

★ ★ ★ The next seven weeks were in a way the worst of all for *Yorktown*. She returned to patrol duty, endlessly sailing back and forth to guard the vital lifeline between America and Australia. It was hot work in those southern seas. "Nowhere in this world," Dutch Schanbacher wrote in his diary, "does the sun rise so brilliantly, burn more brightly, and set so prettily as in the Coral Sea. Here the moon rises swiftly, like a great searchlight, to illuminate the sea."

But *Yorktown* began to feel sorry for herself, and that feeling was accentuated when a rumor spread through the ship that *Lexington* was departing for the States. If true, it would leave *Yorktown* alone in the South Pacific, ringed with enemy ships, planes, and submarines. In truth, *Lexington* was retreating only as far as Pearl Harbor, to have her enormous eight-inch flight-deck gun turrets, holdovers of her conversion from a battle cruiser in the 1920's, replaced with light antiaircraft guns.

Before *Lexington* departed, she and *Yorktown* made a trade. *Yorktown* gave up some of her worn-out planes for an equal number of fresher planes from *Lexington*. In the trade, *Yorktown* was supposed to get six Wildcats; she ended up with only five. Ensign Walt Haas lost the sixth when its engine failed on takeoff. The F4F was the same one that Lieutenant Butch O'Hare had flown when in a single day he had downed the five Japanese bombers off Rabaul. *Yorktown's* mechanics returned to the riddle of the Wildcat malfunctioning. If the problem were not solved, *Yorktown* might end up with no fighter protection at all.

On March 16, *Lexington* and her consorts steamed off to Pearl Harbor, and among *Yorktown's* crew there emerged a certain amount of beefing, not only about *Lexington* but also about *Saratoga*, *Lexington's* sister ship. Just before the war began, *Saratoga* had spent a full year in the Bremerton shipyard, having immense antitorpedo blisters fixed to her sides. Now here she was, back at Bremerton, undergoing extensive repairs for torpedo damage suffered in the Pacific. Yorktowners could scarcely help thinking about *Saratoga's* crew on liberty Stateside while they endured endless watches, heat rash, and saltwater showers.*

The monotony of patrol duty was the worst of it all. Thousands of games of pinochle, cribbage, and acey-deucey were played in tournaments organized by Chaplain Hamilton.

For diversion other Yorktowners began making silver

* Yorktowners chuckled at a malicious cartoon circulated through their ship. It showed *Saratoga*, steaming along encased in her Bremerton dry dock, with a torpedo heading straight for her. A destroyer was racing to intercept the torpedo, but on *Saratoga's* bridge an officer was waving at the destroyer and shouting, "We'll take it! We'll take it!"

rings from fifty-cent pieces. They did it by rotating each coin on its edge and tapping it with a spoon. In time—a long time—the edge flattened out; then a center was bored and filed. *Yorktown's* mess halls eventually ran short of spoons, and Commander Kiefer had to threaten disciplinary action for anyone found in illegal possession of a ship's spoon. Dimes were turned into earrings, and stainless-steel mess trays were used to manufacture wristbands. A number of sailors even took to weaving chenille bedspreads, a square foot at a time, on rude handlooms. And one man spent hundreds of hours covering a one-gallon water jug with an incredibly intricate 105-strand Turk's-head knot.

In the aerology shack, a retreat for *Yorktown's* intellectuals, Joe Doiron argued that birth control was basically immoral. The rebuttal was furnished by a sailor who professed to be a Communist. These thinkers even made tentative plans to buy a farm in Arkansas after the war and turn it into a *Yorktown* cooperative community.

In *Yorktown's* sail loft, Chief Electrician's Mate Walter "Red" Fox, a plank owner (he had been with *Yorktown* since her commissioning), conducted classes in hypnotism. Each pupil paid twenty dollars for the course.

Gambling went on covertly, as it always does. A marathon dice game was played in the CPO washroom, but all the money the men had was forty-two dollars, in one-dollar bills. "When one man had won it all," Chief Cal Callaway later said, "he would parcel it out again, while we kept records of what we owed one another." The temperature in the washroom was always more than 100 degrees, so the money became, in Callaway's words, "so worn and raggedy that we finally had to make a rule that no one could pick it up. Instead, we pushed it around on the deck with a pencil."

Men began to bicker. Chief Petty Officers Bob Powell and Gerald Crowley, both from Boston, argued the merits of East Boston and Dorchester to the point where neither would speak to the other.

The monotony touched even Admiral Fletcher and Captain Buckmaster. One day a passing comment led to a difference of opinion between the two men. The object of the argument was a light switch; the enamel on its cover had been painted so many times that the markings had become indistinguishable.

"I say it says Off-Dim-On," the admiral contended.

"I think you're wrong," the captain said. "I think it goes all the way around and reads Off-On-Off-On."

Admiral Fletcher finally summoned the duty electrician's mate, Gotcher Hampton, to the bridge. "Son," said the admiral, "just what are the readings on that switch?"

"Well," said the nonplussed electrician, "let's have a look, Admiral. Anyone got a knife?"

A knife was produced, and Hampton scraped away nearly a quarter inch of paint, built up over the years. "Looks like you had it right, Captain," he said. Buckmaster smiled; the admiral grunted. The ship sailed on.

Meals became monotonous. Lieutenant Commander Ralph "Bear" Arnold, the supply officer (later to win a Navy Cross for his work as a volunteer gunnery officer), reported to Captain Buckmaster that everything was in short supply except Jello and canned tomatoes. Arnold had a good idea of what the crew thought about the shortages,

for his sleep was regularly interrupted by anonymous telephone calls. "This is the ghost," a voice would tell him,
"the ghost of the poor son of a bitch you starved to death!"

Decent food became an obsession with the crew. Lew
Godfrey and a friend, returning from battle stations one
evening, spotted part of a ham, untended, in the officers'
pantry. They grabbed it and stashed it out of sight in a dis-
mantled radio transmitter. The last ham sandwich, auc-
tioned off, went to Chief Radioman Jim Tindell, who re-
couped most of his money by selling small bites for fifty
cents each.

Seaman Tom Edwards and several others who stood
watch with him on Gun 7 became door shakers. As Edwards told it, "We'd sneak below in the middle of the night
and rattle doorknobs. Whenever we found a door open,
we'd look inside for chow." One night the door shakers
came across an open escape hatch leading to *Yorktown*'s
bakery. They squirmed through the hatch and found scores
of blueberry pies. "Well, I guess we glommed onto thirty
pies," Edwards recalled. "We passed them up the ladder
and tippy-toed through a couple of berthing compartments
with them." Edwards and his friends ate up every pie. The
next morning, before breakfast, the suspects, including Edwards, were ordered into ranks and told to stick out their
tongues. The telltale purplish stain was a dead giveaway.

By early April, *Yorktown*'s freezers were down to the
last five steaks. Chief Pay Clerk P. C. Dahlquist suggested
to Commander Kiefer that they be raffled off.

On April 10 *Yorktown*'s amidships elevator was lowered
to within a few feet of the hangar deck, to serve as a stage,
and the "Yorktown Jamboree" began. The steaks were

paraded around the deck under armed Marine guard. Then the show began.* Acts included Seaman Sidney Flum as "Miss Fanny Flum, the Only Bearded Lady Jitterbug in Captivity." Chief Walter Fox, "The Swami of Granby Street," doubled as master of ceremonies and hypnotist, and in no time at all he had six shipmates mesmerized, wading and swimming around the deck, whipping out of clothing they thought was afire, and eating onions they saw as oranges.

As the evening's finale, the names of the raffle winners were drawn from a box. The winners were seated at an elaborately arranged table. A "waitress"—John Underwood, a fourteen-year-old in Fighting 42 who had lied about his age to get into the Navy—served the sizzling steaks. His breasts were two soup bowls, his blond hair was a wig made from an unraveled section of hawser, and his delicate white knee-length hose had been borrowed from a British naval observer.

After the show, it was back to work and a dreary diet cycle of baked beans, canned Vienna sausage, canned corned beef, canned salmon, and chipped beef and rice.

Not long after the steak raffle, the mystery of the defective Wildcat fighter planes was finally solved. The trouble was traced to the quality of aviation fuel with which *Yorktown* had been supplied and the self-sealing gasoline tanks in the airplanes. The fuel, apparently of a lower quality than that which *Yorktown* had received in prewar days, was eating away the rubber tank liners, and tiny bits of

---

* Captain Buckmaster did not attend; after *Yorktown* departed Pearl Harbor, he rarely left the bridge. All his meals were brought to him on a tray, and he used no lights after dusk for fear of affecting his night vision.

rubber were finding their way into the airplanes' carburetors, choking the engines.

A plane was flown to the nearest friendly island, from which there was relayed to Pearl Harbor a message requesting that replacement liners be sent immediately and that *Yorktown* be allowed to put into port somewhere for upkeep and replenishment. Back came a reply (also indirectly, because *Yorktown* was maintaining radio silence) stating that new tank liners would soon be on their way. An accompanying message that outraged *Yorktown's* officers expressed amazement that *Yorktown* would "retreat in the face of the enemy." Members of Fletcher's staff urged the admiral to send an acid rejoinder. But Fletcher, wise in the ways of command staffs and certain of the identity of the man who had drafted the offending message, cautioned patience. A few days later, he received a more reasonable message and, with it, orders to put into Tongatabu, in the Friendly Islands, for a week.

At 12:12 P.M. on April 20, *Yorktown* moored in Nukualofa Anchorage, off an island that Ensign John Lorenz ecstatically described as "right out of Nordhoff and Hall." Red Fox's hypnotism students chortled to one another as they anticipated using their newly acquired skills on unsuspecting island females.

As the first liberty boat neared shore, Fireman George Domienik let out a delighted cry. "Just like the movies!" he said. "All those natives are bare from the waist up!" But all the natives he had seen were men, most of them 6 feet tall and weighing more than 200 pounds. They were members of the island's constabulary. Queen Salote, the widow giantess who ruled the island nation, had removed nearly all the young women to remote inland hideaways.

There was practically nothing to buy on the island, a disappointment to Yorktowners, for the day they arrived was payday. One Yorktowner, Boatswain's Mate John Sharp, took all his pay ashore with him and came back with but one purchase—a can of heat-rash powder. A brisk business did develop in tropical fruit. Yorktowners ate all the bananas they could hold and took an additional supply back with them to the ship. "For days after in the engine room," George Bateman recalled, "you could pluck bananas like they were hanging on trees. We had them hanging in stalks from the overhead." A few Yorktowners managed to find women, who recognized no U.S. dollar denomination less than twenty dollars. One intrepid Yankee, according to Leroy Gill, did manage to pass off prewar cigar coupons as legal tender.

As these Yorktowners were gamboling the best they could at Tongatabu, the Imperial Japanese Navy continued to build on its already impressive fighting record and, at the same time, to improve its tactics.

In the Indian Ocean, Vice Admiral Chuichi Nagumo worked to eliminate what major opposition still remained. His carriers had perfected an unbeatable technique: they would send off one strike wave of dive bombers, torpedo planes, and fighters, immediately positioning a second comparable force on the flight decks. As a new target was discovered, the second wave would be launched. Since Japanese carriers carried a plentiful supply of fighter planes, there were always sufficient Zeros remaining to protect the ships against attack while both forces were away. On one occasion a second wave sank the British cruisers *Dorsetshire* and *Cornwall*; on another, a second wave sank the British carrier *Hermes* and the destroyer *Vampire*. By April 10, British strength in the Indian Ocean had shriveled to a few old battleships, and they—stripped of air cover—retreated to Madagascar. When Nagumo decided that his work was done, he headed for home. En route, he detached from his Carrier Division 5, centered around the big new carriers *Zuikaku* and *Shokaku*, and ordered them to Truk Island in the Carolines. There they were to stand by for another planned Japanese move.*

In four short months, by mid-April Japan had achieved all her initial military objectives. It was time, Japanese naval planners thought, to move into the second phase, to invade Australia. They reasoned, quite properly, that no serious counterattack could be launched against them from any other quarter. However, Army planners demurred. Winter snows were melting on the Asian mainland, and the Russian-German conflict was still in doubt. If they weakened their Manchuria and Korea garrisons to supply troops in the south, they might find Russian soldiers streaming in on those defenses from the north.

A compromise was reached. The Imperial Army would provide a limited force to work with the Imperial Navy, to take the Solomon Islands, and New Guinea. That would give them control of the air over the Coral Sea. They would

---

* Eight days later, on April 18, Army Lieutenant Colonel James Doolittle's B-25 bombers rumbled off the carrier *Hornet's* deck to strike at the Japanese homeland. This daring and unexpected move gave an enormous lift to American morale, especially when President Roosevelt told a mystified public that the attack had been launched from "Shangri-La," the mythical Tibetan retreat of James Hilton's novel *Lost Horizon*. This explanation so captured the nation's imagination that an aircraft carrier then under construction was given that name. *Hornet*, accompanied by *Enterprise*, returned to Pearl Harbor.

then strike at Midway and the western Aleutians, thus bringing the U.S. fleet into a decisive engagement. Finally, they would move against New Caledonia, Fiji, and Samoa. Australia, even if it remained unoccupied, would thereby be effectively isolated.

It was a reasonable plan. The only trouble was that Admiral Chester Nimitz knew about it. Not long before, American intelligence had broken the Japanese naval code, just as the Japanese diplomatic code had been broken in 1941.

On April 29 (Admiral Fletcher's birthday, as well as Emperor Hirohito's), *Yorktown* received word that *Lexington,* her new antiaircraft guns installed, was again at sea. *Lexington*'s task force, commanded by Rear Admiral Aubrey Fitch, was to join the *Yorktown* force, both forces to be under the command of Admiral Fletcher. Also steaming to join the combined force was Rear Admiral John C. Crace, Royal Australian Navy, with two cruisers.

Fletcher's orders were simple enough; by May 1 he was to start operating with his combined force in the Coral Sea. Somehow he had to stop the Japanese from taking Port Moresby, the essential Allied forward base on the southern coast of the Papua Peninsula on New Guinea.

The Japanese thrust was divided into six forces:

1. The Tulagi invasion force was to run southeast down the Solomons chain from Rabaul, take Tulagi, and set up a seaplane base there. This force was made up of one large transport, two destroyers, and a number of minesweepers and submarine chasers. From the seaplane base at Tulagi, the immense Japanese Kawanishi flying boats would be able to cover the entire eastern reaches of the Coral Sea.

2. The Misima Island support group—composed of two light cruisers, a seaplane carrier, and three gunboats—was to set up a second seaplane base at Misima Island, off New Guinea's eastern tip, before the invasion of Port Moresby. From that base, flying boats would be able to cover the western reaches of the Coral Sea.

3. The Port Moresby invasion group—composed of five transports; assorted minelayers, minesweepers, and oilers; and a defensive screen of six destroyers—was to sail from Rabaul, round the eastern tip of New Guinea, and land invasion troops at Port Moresby.

4. The Port Moresby covering group, made up of the light carrier *Shoho*, accompanied by four heavy cruisers, was to stand off Port Moresby and protect the invasion convoy.

5. The carrier task force—composed of the two big modern carriers *Zuikaku* and *Shokaku*, carrying a total of forty-two fighter planes, forty-one dive bombers, and forty-two torpedo planes, along with two heavy cruisers, six destroyers, and an oiler—was to deal with American carriers should they try to interfere with the landing operation.

6. The land-based air flotilla, with nearly 150 Japanese naval aircraft, based at Rabaul, was under orders to back up the ships at sea whenever they were needed. With a range of 600 miles, these planes could reach out to Tulagi and Port Moresby and anything in between.

According to the Japanese timetable, Tulagi was to be occupied on May 3. The Port Moresby invasion group was to leave Rabaul on May 4 and begin going ashore on May 7. Naturally, the Japanese expected that the Americans would try to intervene. When they did appear, they would be attacked by the covering group (centered on the light carrier *Shoho*) from the west and the big strike force (the carriers *Zuikaku* and *Shokaku*) from the east. The Americans would be caught in a pincer and destroyed. That job finished, the carriers would attack Allied air bases in northern Australia, and the Tulagi invasion group would move northeast to occupy the islands of Ocean and Nauru.

Unlike the Japanese, the Americans consolidated their strength. It included, first of all, the carriers *Yorktown* and *Lexington,* supported by six American cruisers, two Australian cruisers, thirteen destroyers, two oilers, and a seaplane tender. In addition, there were the 484 Army bombers and fighters in Australia, but they all were under the command of General MacArthur and thus might or might not be available for naval use.

Enterprise and *Hornet* were the remaining two U.S. carriers in the western Pacific, and they were at Pearl Harbor, just back from Doolittle's B-25 strike against Japan. It is more than 3,000 miles from Pearl Harbor to the Coral Sea, and even if they were rushed to sea, they would surely be too late. The only other force in the Pacific was Task Force 1, at San Francisco, made up entirely of ancient battleships, and no one could see what use it would be in the coming action.

Thus, Admiral Nimitz was forced to rely on what he had; there was simply nothing else available to him. Nimitz would issue the combat orders; the rest would be up to Black Jack Fletcher, in *Yorktown.*

Chapter Five

* * * * * * *

* * * Official Navy records show that May 1 was the day *Lexington* and *Yorktown* joined forces, under orders to "destroy enemy ships, shipping, and aircraft at favorable opportunities in order to assist in checking further advance by enemy in the New Guinea-Solomons area." Members of *Yorktown*'s crew recall that May 1 was also the day that *Yorktown* ran out of toilet paper. A substitute for that personal need could be found; but there was no substitute for fuel oil, and so *Yorktown*, the same morning, began taking fuel from the tanker *Neosho*. *Lexington*, a few miles away, began filling up from another oiler, *Tippecanoe*, whose kindly supply officer saw to it that *Yorktown*'s other more delicate need was also met.

At 3:17 P.M., *Yorktown* was still refueling when Lieutenant (jg) Stanley "Stan" Vetjasa of Scouting 5, flying patrol with Ensign H. N. Ervin as wingman, spotted a Japanese submarine. As the I-boat dived, Vetjasa carefully noted her position and, maintaining radio silence, flew back over *Yorktown* and dropped a message on her deck. Three torpedo bombers were loaded with depth charges and hurried aloft to track down the submarine.

The TBDs sighted the submarine at 4:15 P.M., some twenty-five miles from *Yorktown*. She had, postwar information revealed, already radioed the whereabouts of *Yorktown* to Rabaul. The three bombers dropped six depth bombs along the path the submarine was following (the water was so clear that the fliers could actually see the submarine's outline). The pilots, returning to *Yorktown*, reported that the depth bombs had exploded close enough to the submarine to sink her or at least to register serious damage. But in fact, the submarine escaped undamaged, and the Japanese—for the first time in seventy-five days— knew *Yorktown*'s precise location.

Somehow the message was never relayed from Rabaul to the Japanese ships at sea searching for *Yorktown*. The Japanese command structure was rather bizarre, with land commands not specifically bound to obey sea commands and vice versa. There was no overall boss of the sweeping operation, so that no one in Rabaul felt duty-bound to pass the word along.

Fletcher, in *Yorktown*, believing he had been discovered, headed northwest toward the tip of New Guinea, hoping to find the Japanese transports and sink them before he came under attack. But *Lexington* and her escorts were still taking on fuel; Fletcher was forced to leave them behind, with instructions to join him two days later, at daylight on May 4. Admiral Crace and his cruisers were to rendezvous then, too.

On the following day, May 2, Army B-17s spotted a Japanese force heading for Tulagi, but the information—reminiscent of Japanese slackness—failed to reach Fletcher until twenty-six hours later. When, on May 3, he did get the word, Fletcher decided he could not wait a day for *Lexington* to catch up; he would have to move alone against Tulagi. He instructed the destroyer *Sims* and the tanker *Neosho* to keep the rendezvous appointment with *Lexington* and the Australian cruisers and to inform them that he was attacking. By 8:30 P.M. on May 3, *Yorktown*, accompanied by four cruisers and six destroyers, had turned north and was making twenty-four knots toward Guadalcanal.

Captain Buckmaster called Radioman Vane Bennett, *Yorktown's* radar expert, to the bridge and told him that a Japanese task force was on the prowl. He ordered Bennett to double the radar watch and to remain stationed near the equipment at all times. "The captain told me I could lie down on some life jackets in a corner and get some sleep if my eyes got too blurry," Bennett recalled later.

Yorktown pilots were eager for action but puzzled when told of Japanese ships off Tulagi. They had never heard of the place. "Finally," one of them reported, "we were shown what the place looked like, from a copy of an old *National Geographic* magazine." Night-before plans included being given a bearing along which to fly that would take them over Guadalcanal Island on a south-to-north heading. Tulagi and the enemy ships should then be in sight straight ahead.

At 7 A.M. on May 4, *Yorktown*, about fifty miles south of Guadalcanal, put up an umbrella of six Wildcats (they had received new fuel tank self-sealers at Tongatabu). Then, at 7:30, *Yorktown* began launching a strike—twelve torpedo bombers under Lieutenant Commander Joe Taylor, thirteen dive bombers under Lieutenant Commander Bill

Burch, and another fifteen dive bombers under Lieutenant Wally Short. At 8:45 A.M. they were in sight of the enemy, and the five-day Battle of the Coral Sea was begun.

Off Tulagi were a Japanese transport, two destroyers, and nine auxiliary ships. Commander Burch and eight other SBDs of Scouting 5 dived on them. Halfway down, Burch thought he saw a cruiser and two destroyers nesting together; he shifted the direction of the attack toward them.

This sudden change in direction, along with a repetition of the fogging of bombsights and windshields that had plagued the same bombers at New Guinea, reduced the attack's effectiveness. Still, when it was over, Burch was sure that his men had scored a number of hits.

Joe Taylor and Torpedo 5 went in next, circling the targets to approach them from the direction of the shore. Ed Williamson, an enlisted pilot, asked for and received permission to break off and make his attack from still another direction. Keeping well to the left of the Japanese ships, he flew over Tulagi, came about, and made his run so that his TBD was bow to bow with the nested ships. Williamson's torpedo struck the center ship, while his radioman, Joe Crawford, strafed enthusiastically as the TBD broke away. All the other torpedo bombers, even though they had made their runs with little or no enemy interference, missed their targets.

Watching the attack from above the action was Commander Walter "Butch" Schindler, ordnance officer on Fletcher's staff. He had been sent along, doubling as rear gunner for Ensign Hugh Nicholson, to make the coldest, most objective kind of appraisal. "It was a disappointing sight," he later recalled, "to see all those torpedo wakes crisscrossing the harbor and exploding against the beaches." The trouble really was not so much the pilots as it was the torpedoes. Their failure at Tulagi was to be experienced again and again, until pilots could rightly argue that the Navy's inability to produce an adequate torpedo was nothing short of a scandal.

Of the two strikes so far that day, little or no damage had been inflicted against the enemy. Next in was Bombing 5—composed of more dive bombers. They, too, had the same frustrating problem of sight reduced because of fogging. The best they could report was that two pilots, Joseph "Jo-Jo" Powers and Leif Larsen, had probably scored hits. As the planes made for their poststrike rendezvous, a single float-equipped Zero rose to challenge them. Nearly all of Bombing 5's rear gunners, including Commander Schindler, blazed away at him. Finally, he spun away in flames.

At 10 A.M. all planes were back aboard *Yorktown,* and the only damage anyone could find was a small-caliber bullet hole in the aileron of Ensign G. E. Bottjer's dive bomber. This was cause for rejoicing indeed, but when all the reports of returning pilots were put together, it became clear that the overall attack in general had been a failure.

Fletcher may have had his failings, but he also had what every great commander must have—the will to engage the enemy, again and again. At 11:06 A.M. he sent off another strike. Lieutenant Wally Short and fourteen dive bombers were away first. When they arrived over Tulagi, they found the sound between that island and Guadalcanal nearly empty of targets. Had they, after all, sunk all the

Japanese ships the first time around? Hardly. A few minutes later they spotted what appeared to be three gunboats and a seaplane tender hightailing it towards Rabaul. Short's dive bombers attacked and in a matter of minutes sank two of the gunboats. As the bombers peeled away to strafe Tulagi, the third also appeared to be sinking.

Bill Burch's thirteen dive bombers were close behind Short's squadron. They found a destroyer and reported later that they had hit it twice. During the attack a single-engine seaplane fighter rose to challenge them. Burch reported that the seaplane's rear gunner kept shooting every minute, even when the ungainly plane was coming out of rolls and turns. It required nearly 3,000 rounds of machine gun fire from the thirteen bombers to kill off the single seaplane. Yorktowners, more than ever before, began to appreciate the enemy's flying skill.

Yorktown's cumbersome torpedo planes were launched last, and they, too, found a Japanese destroyer. Six of the TBDs approached her from one side; five, from the other. It was a textbook attack. "We had a dream torpedo pattern," Ed Williamson, one of the pilots, recalled. "But every single fish missed the stinker." It was no fault of *Yorktown's*. Depth settings of the torpedoes had been double- and triple-checked prior to takeoff. Every one of them apparently ran far too deep.

Last in line among the torpedo planes was the TBD piloted by Lieutenant Leonard "Spike" Ewoldt, whose radioman was Ray Machalinski. Ewoldt lined up against a Japanese destroyer and started his run. But when he tried to release the torpedo electrically, nothing happened. "We're going around again," he told Machalinski. The second time, Ewoldt reached down and yanked the manual release. The torpedo fell away, but of course, it also ran too deep.

Pulling clear of the destroyer, Ewoldt looked around for the other torpedo planes; all of them had disappeared. He missed the rendezvous and then, in the foggy weather, missed *Yorktown*, too. Gasoline almost gone, he had no choice but to ditch his plane. He and Machalinski crawled out of the plane, inflated their life raft, and waited for a rescue ship. The first ship to appear, however, was a Japanese destroyer, but it steamed right past them. Hours later a friendly sea washed them up on Guadalcanal's southern shore. Natives and missionaries found them and somehow kept them one step ahead of Japanese search parties. Ultimately, they were given a small boat, an old sextant, a worn star almanac, and some hand-drawn charts. Two months after going down off Guadalcanal, they put safely into Efate in the New Hebrides.

Yorktown had also launched four Wildcats to cover the bombers and torpedo planes over Tulagi. The pilots were Bill Leonard, Ed Bassett, Scotty McCuskey, and John Adams.

"You know," McCuskey recalled later, "I wasn't even supposed to go. I was just moving the aircraft on the flight deck for a pilot who hadn't finished his lunch. Then, all of a sudden, away we went." McCuskey and Adams were, it should be remembered, *Yorktown*'s original heroes; they had registered the first kill in shooting down a Kawanishi flying boat in the Gilbert Islands.

Passing over Guadalcanal, Bassett and Leonard encountered three Zero float planes. Leonard went after one of them, but the enemy wheeled and came at him head on. Just when it seemed that the two planes would collide, the Zero pulled up, nosed over, and dived past Leonard straight into the sea. Bassett, meanwhile, had chased and gunned down one of the two other Zeros. The third, amid the confusion, latched onto Leonard's tail. Leonard gave his Wildcat full throttle, wheeled around, and came roaring back at the Zero in another nose-to-nose confrontation. The Zero ducked under him, pulled into a sharp climb, spun over on one wing, and plunged into the sea. Bassett and Leonard agreed later that the action had lasted no more than three minutes.

McCuskey and Adams, for their part, came upon a Japanese gunboat and chased it up on a beach. Later they spotted the Japanese destroyer *Yuzuki* and began giving it the same kind of treatment. In the midst of their attack they were joined by Bassett and Leonard. The four Wildcats pumped 4,000 rounds into the destroyer, killing its captain and dozens of its crew. However, it got away, severely but not mortally hurt.

Bassett and Leonard made it back to *Yorktown,* but McCuskey and Adams, eager to find more targets, flew around until they ran low on gas. Like Ewoldt, they had to ditch their planes. The two fighter pilots landed on the southern shore of Guadalcanal and rigged a tent from one of their parachutes. The destroyer *Hammann* spotted the tent and swung out a boat to rescue the two pilots. The surf, however, was too heavy for the whaleboat to make a landing, so Coxswain George Kapp, a line in his hand, leaped into the sea and swam to shore. He hooked the line to the pilots' life raft, then climbed aboard with McCuskey and Adams. All three men were hauled out to the whaleboat.

Following the launching of the four Wildcats, *Yorktown* put a third strike aloft. Nine of its dive bombers found a cargo ship north of Savo Island; two hits were recorded. The other twelve dive bombers, led by the redoubtable Bill Burch, found two ships off Tulagi. One of them, a small craft, was sunk.

By 4:30 P.M. all of *Yorktown*'s planes, except the two Wildcats and Ewoldt's torpedo bomber, were back aboard; the strike against Tulagi was over. Once again, results were disappointing. *Yorktown* aircraft, according to the official action report, had launched twenty-three torpedoes and had dropped seventy-six 1,000-pound bombs.

Yorktown now steamed to the south, to keep the appointment with *Lexington* and the Australian cruiser. The Japanese were also on the move. Their invasion force was already several hours out of Rabaul, with the two big carriers *Zuikaku* and *Shokaku* north of the Solomons, heading south from Truk. When they learned of *Yorktown*'s activities, they turned on speed and headed around the eastern end of the island chain, hoping to catch up with the American ships. And they might have done just that, for Fletcher had at one point decided to send his cruisers and several destroyers around Guadalcanal "to clean up Tulagi." But he had had second thoughts about it, which was just as well for him.

At 8:46 A.M. on May 5 (the day Japanese soldiers stormed ashore on Corregidor Island in the Philippines),

Admirals Fletcher, Fitch, and Crace rendezvoused. An uninvited guest, one of the ubiquitous Kawanishi flying boats, also showed up. Four *Yorktown* pilots—Ed Mattson, Vince McCormack, Walt Haas, and Art Brassfield— began to track it down. Brassfield attacked first, coming in from the right. McCormack came in next from the left. Walt Haas, third, came in right behind McCormack. Just as Mattson was preparing to make his run, the flying boat began trailing smoke from all four engines. The smoke soon turned into flame, and the Kawanishi began a long, gentle, flaming glide into the ocean. The action lasted thirty seconds and required only 260 bullets.

For Fletcher and Buckmaster, May 5 was a day of interlude, a day to put the pieces together. While *Yorktown* again refueled from *Neosho*, Fletcher studied intelligence reports, from which, he concluded, it was obvious that the Japanese were clustering a large number of ships, including at least three aircraft carriers, near New Britain, the Solomons, and New Guinea. He reasoned that the Japanese would probably try to establish a seaplane base off New Guinea's eastern tip, from which they could keep a lookout for the American carriers. He anticipated also that the invasion convoy would try to slip through Jomard Passage, off the eastern tip of New Guinea, in order to get at Port Moresby.

On the same day, when Fletcher received word that U.S. Army planes had sighted a Japanese carrier in the area, he halted the refueling and, at 7:30 P.M., headed northwest again. Besides *Yorktown*, the American fleet included *Lexington*, eight cruisers, and eleven destroyers.

Yorktown, on May 5, had been out of Pearl Harbor for

eighty days without meaningful relief or replenishment. Seaman Russell Brown, who had charge of *Yorktown's* clothing store, reported that his stock "was down to nothing but some black socks and a few white shirts with size seventeen and a half and eighteen collars." The crew was literally getting ragged. And the ship itself, which had once had a reputation as a showboat, was beginning to look ragged, too.

May 6 dawned, and still neither side knew the position of enemy forces. At 7:30 A.M., Fletcher formally combined his force, Admiral Fitch's force, and Crace's cruisers into Task Force 17. On paper, he divided his escorts into two groups. One, under Admiral Crace, would be assigned to attack the invasion convoy once it was sighted. The other would remain with the two carriers as a protective screen.

Fletcher had no way of knowing it, but the Japanese were closing in. *Shoho,* the light carrier, was preparing to weigh anchor in the Shortland Islands. The Japanese troop-ships were a day out of Rabaul, and the two big carriers, *Zuikaku* and *Shokaku,* had rounded the Solomons and were coming up, behind Fletcher.

At 10:30 A.M. high-flying Army B-17s sighted *Shoho* and tried to bomb her. They missed. In their official report the pilots reported that they had come close to hitting "light cruisers." An hour later other B-17s sighted the invasion convoy. (Thirty minutes earlier, a Japanese plane had sighted Fletcher, but the word was once again not passed to the Japanese ship commanders.) Before the afternoon was over, Fletcher had decided on a series of moves. He sent *Neosho* south, with the destroyer *Sims* as escort, to wait for the carriers at the next refueling rendezvous. Then, convinced that the Japanese invasion convoy would start through Jomard Passage at the eastern tail of New Guinea the next day, he ordered both his carriers to prepare for an attack.

The Battle of the Coral Sea, the first great naval battle since Jutland, was building to a climax, and Yorktowners knew that it was.

Hangar- and flight-deck crews gassed the aircraft, and ordnancemen broke out bombs, hanging them from aircraft bellies. Torpedomen went over each fish, checking its detonator and the air pressure in its flask. Gunner's mates checked their ready ammunition lockers and exercised their guns. Fire controlmen removed range finder covers and wiped the lenses clear with soft tissue paper. Signalmen checked their flag bags to be sure all halyards, hooks, and rings were clear for free running so that signal hoists could be snapped to yardarms smartly.

All this did not take long. Yorktowners had already gone on the run to their battle stations more than 160 times since they had departed Pearl Harbor. Battle stations had been cleared of loose gear, and the men knew their assignments. By the time the evening meal was finished, they were as ready as they would ever be.

Many Yorktowners stayed up late. Ship's Cook Renzie Cardin, who had the late galley watch, recalled that dozens of them came in for coffee and sandwiches. "And for once," he wrote later, "they didn't complain to me about food. All their talk was about wives and sweethearts and families."

Storekeeper Tom Callaghan stayed up late, working. He checked the record of every man in Fighting 42 for pay allotments and GI insurance. When he turned in, Callaghan's mind was at ease—every man who could be persuaded to do so had made provision for his family back home. The pay records served as legal proof of it.

Lieutenant Commander Hubie Strange, studying the weather reports, liked what he saw. As things stood, *Yorktown* was protected by a weather front. But when dawn broke, the enemy should, he believed, be nicely exposed under clear skies just beyond the weather front's northern edge.

Chapter Six

★ ★ ★ ★ ★ ★ ★

★ ★ ★ Hubie Strange, *Yorktown's* weather officer, had called it neatly. At 6:15 A.M. on May 7, 1942, the day the Battle of the Coral Sea began in earnest, *Yorktown* was running through rainsqualls under thick cloud cover, but the weather was broken sufficiently to allow the carrier to launch ten dive bombers. They had orders from Lieutenant Commander Oscar Pederson, who had become *Yorktown's* air group commander, to search an area, northwest to east, for a distance of 250 miles.

The bombers were hardly over the horizon when Admiral Fletcher detached Admiral Crace with three cruisers and three destroyers. Fletcher expected that as many as a dozen Japanese troopships would be attempting to slip through Jomard Passage, and he hoped that Crace could find them and sink them.*

---

* Professor Morison, in his *History of United States Naval Operations in World War II*, questions this decision. By dispatching Crace, Morison argues, Fletcher weakened his own antiaircraft screen. Moreover, if Fletcher had won, he would have had ample time to destroy the Japanese convoy. If he had lost, Crace would surely have been chewed up. Coral Sea, however, was the first big battle, and U.S. tactics were still evolving. Fletcher understood the risk involved, but he also recognized that his only purpose off New Guinea was to sink those Japanese transports. He meant to do it. Port Moresby had to be protected at whatever cost.

At 5:45 A.M. a search group had been launched from the two big Japanese carriers, *Zuikaku* and *Shokaku*, both well to the east of *Yorktown*. At 7:30 one of these planes spotted the slow, waddling oiler *Neosho* and her escort destroyer, *Sims*.

The Japanese pilot mistook the broad flat oiler for an aircraft carrier, an error that would prove generally costly to the Japanese and particularly devastating to *Neosho* and *Sims*. Rear Admiral Tadaichi Hara, commander of the Japanese carrier division, ordered an immediate strike against these two relatively minor targets, which were hundreds of miles away from *Yorktown* and *Lexington*, Hara's real quarry.

Japanese planes dropped three 500-pound bombs on *Sims*; she sank within minutes. *Neosho* was hit seven times but somehow remained afloat. (Rescue ships finally located her on May 11, took off the survivors, and scuttled her.)

While the Japanese were concentrating on the wrong targets, Fletcher was having his own troubles locating the enemy. At 7:35 A.M. one of the ten dive bombers *Yorktown* had launched at 6:15 reported that it had sighted two Japanese cruisers well to the northwest of *Yorktown*. Ten minutes later, Lieutenant John Neilsen, searching a nearby sector, encountered a float-equipped scout from one of the cruisers accompanying the old carrier *Shoho*. He shot it down. Later, Ensign Lloyd Bigelow met a carrier-based torpedo plane and shot it down.

At 8:15 A.M., just after the seventy-eight-plane strike had roared away from *Zuikaku* and *Shokaku* for *Neosho* and *Sims*, a *Yorktown* pilot made another sighting report. He radioed that he had two carriers and four cruisers in view, all of 'them northwest of *Yorktown*. This, Fletcher concluded, was what he had been waiting for. He ordered *Yorktown's* Buckmaster and *Lexington's* Admiral Frederick C. "Ted" Sherman to launch strikes against them immediately.

Fifteen minutes later, *Yorktown's* radar picked up a nearby snooper. Wildcats were sent after it, but the Japanese pilot skipped from cloud to cloud; aboard *Yorktown*, radio interceptors heard him make his report of their position. By 9 A.M. Fletcher was convinced that the Japanese carrier commanders knew his whereabouts, and he was correct. What Fletcher did not know was that Vice Admiral Shigeyoshi Inouye, commander of Japan's 4th Fleet, had become so disturbed by the presence of the two American carriers that he had ordered the Port Moresby invasion convoy to turn back. Admiral Inouye, land-based at Rabaul, reasoned that the convoy could wait out of harm's way until the American carriers were destroyed, after which the invasion could be resumed.

At 9:25 A.M. planes began taking off from *Yorktown* and *Lexington* in a powerful strike against two Japanese carriers and four cruisers that had been sighted a little more than an hour earlier. The ninety-four planes from the two carriers were heading north at 10:13, *Lexington's* planes slightly in the lead. All that was left behind aboard *Yorktown* were nine Wildcats, a dive bomber that Lieutenant J. W. "Win" Rowley had been unable to get started, and two inoperative torpedo bombers. Still aloft, but not part of the strike, were the ten scout bombers that had been searching for the Japanese carriers. *Lexington* retained

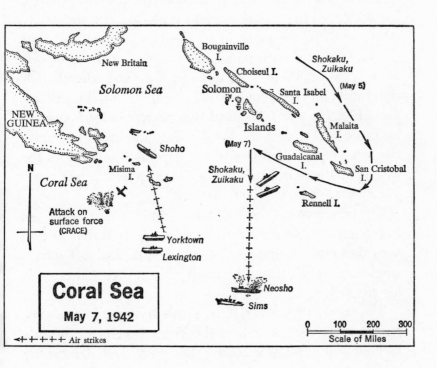

New Britain

Solomon Sea

Bougainville I.

Choiseul I.

Solomon

Santa Isabel I.

Shokaku, Zuikaku

(May 5)

NEW GUINEA

Islands

Malaita I.

Shoho

(May 7)

Misima I.

Guadalcanal I.

San Cristobal I.

N

Coral Sea

Shokaku, Zuikaku

Attack on surface force (CRACE)

Rennell I.

Yorktown

Lexington

Coral Sea

May 7, 1942

Neosho

Sims

0   100   200   300

Scale of Miles

┽┼┼┼┼ Air strikes

eight of her Wildcats for air defense, plus eight bombers for antisubmarine defense.

At 10:22 A.M. an Army B-17 reported that it had sighted an aircraft carrier, ten transports, and sixteen other ships. As Fletcher read the report, it sounded authentic enough, but it showed the enemy carrier's position to be some sixty miles south of the position of the two carriers and four cruisers the *Yorktown* plane had reported. If both reports were accurate, there were not two but three aircraft carriers north of *Yorktown*. From available intelligence reports Fletcher was convinced that he was indeed opposed by three enemy carriers, but he was equally certain from the same reports that two of the carriers should be to the east or northeast of him, in which case somebody had made a mistake. Whom was he to believe?

The dilemma was resolved a few minutes later, when the *Yorktown* scout landed and the pilot reported that he had seen two cruisers and four destroyers; he had not seen a single carrier. How had he made such a dreadful error in his report?

The explanation was simple. While trying to keep an eye on the enemy ships and, at the same time, to maintain a lookout for enemy planes, the pilot had incorrectly matched the two circular sections of his encoding board. The radioman, taking his information from the pilot, had reported "two carriers" instead of "two cruisers" and "four cruisers" instead of "four destroyers."

Fortunately, there was still time to redirect the *Yorktown-Lexington* strike to the position reported by the Army B-17. Such orders crackled from *Yorktown* at 10:53 A.M.

Lexington's planes made contact with the enemy's ships

first. Troopships were nowhere in sight (they had, of course, been turned back), but there was one large carrier below—*Shoho,* a 14,000-tonner—escorted by four cruisers and a destroyer. *Shoho* twisted and turned as best she could as twenty-seven dive bombers from *Lexington* came down after her. This simple evasiveness was enough; *Lexington*'s planes made only a single hit, with what appeared to be a bomb that took *Shoho* in the stern.

As things now developed, *Lexington*'s torpedo planes (Torpedo 2) and dive bombers from *Yorktown* (Scouting 5) joined in a simultaneous attack, although it had not been planned that way. Torpedo 2 scored three hits on *Shoho*'s port side, the other torpedoes either missed or ran wild. Lieutenant Commander Bill Burch's sixteen dive bombers came pounding in and hit *Shoho* twelve times. Lieutenant Stan Vetjasa was immediately behind Burch. "The skipper laid one right in the middle of her flight deck," Vetjasa reported. "It was a beauty. I got a hit right after that. So did Hugh Nicholson, Art Downing, Roger Woodhull, and Charlie Ware."

Yorktown's Scouting 5 had scarcely pulled away when Bombing 5 came in. Four of the pilots—Jo-Jo Powers, Win Rowley, Bill Christie, and Ben Preston—scored hits. "I was second to last of our twenty-seven dive bombers," Preston recalled. "By the time I pushed over, the carrier— we thought she was the *Ryukaku* at the time—was burning like mad. Flames were pouring out from under her flight deck, all along both sides of the ship."

The last of Bombing 5's planes was breaking away when Lieutenant Commander Joe Taylor went in with ten of *Yorktown*'s torpedo bombers. They spread out as they approached *Shoho,* formed a long arc along her starboard side, and then turned and arrowed in, using *Shoho's* island structure as a target.

"There never was so successful a torpedo pattern in the entire war, I believe," claimed Tom Ellison, one of the pilots. "We went in at fifty or sixty feet altitude against hardly any antiaircraft fire and launched from as close as six hundred feet." Ellison, who did not trust the electrical torpedo release, yanked hard on the manual release. He saw his torpedo boring straight for *Shoho* as he turned away. *Shoho* by then was so crippled that she could not evade the swarm of attackers.

Ed Williamson went in on *Shoho's* starboard bow. He fired all the ammunition from his fixed machine guns, kicking rudder pedals now and then "to sort of spray ahead of me." Then he released his torpedo; it and three others from the ten attacking Yorktowners caught *Shoho* along her starboard side. With such an easy target, the fish that missed almost surely were defective.

Williamson, one of the last to attack, banked hard over to fly clear of the area. "I settled on a course for our rendezvous position," he reported. "I took a quick look around for bogeys, then decided to check the target. Darned if the thing wasn't gone!"

Gone she was indeed. Lieutenant Commander Bob Dixon, skipper of *Lexington's* Scouting 2, was so excited about the kill that he broke radio silence. "Scratch one flattop!" he shouted. *Shoho* was still making twenty knots when, witnesses said, she went right under. She had been destroyed by ninety-four planes in twenty-one minutes, taking more than 800 men to the bottom with her.

Shoho had known the attack was coming and had managed to get off a few fighters. Some of them went after Burch's dive bombers, some after Taylor's torpedo planes. *Yorktown* fighters under Lieutenant Commander Jimmy Flatley shielded the torpedo planes; they shot down three Japanese planes and chased away a fourth.

Commander Butch Schindler was once again observing the action as Admiral Fletcher's personal emissary; this time, he was Stan Vetjasa's gunner. When the Japanese fighters came swarming in, Schindler—who had been having trouble with gun jamming—managed to get off a burst that downed one of the attackers.

Win Rowley, the dive bomber pilot, became so exasperated with a Japanese fighter that he called to his gunner, Seaman Demon Musgrove, "What do you say we go get that guy?" Rowley peeled off after one of the enemy fighters and chased it away. But when the chase was finished, Rowley found himself all alone and low on gas. He broke radio silence to inform *Yorktown* of his predicament, but the carrier either did not get the message or, to preserve its anonymity, refused to answer. Rowley spotted an Australian ship a few minutes later; Musgrove talked to it by blinker lamp to obtain information on distance and direction to Port Moresby. But the plane ran out of fuel miles short of the goal, and Rowley had to ditch. He and Musgrove drifted ashore, where they were protected by friendly natives, and eventually made their way to Australia.

At 1:09 P.M., *Yorktown* and *Lexington* began recovering their planes. Commander Dixon's violation of strict radio silence had done no harm, for it allowed both carriers to clear their flight decks for landings, instead of spotting a new strike force on them.

Yorktown could not help being pleased with what she had accomplished. Her planes could take credit for 90 percent of the sinking *Shoho* and the planes that went down with her and for seven more planes shot from the sky.*

By 2 P.M., *Yorktown's* planes were ready to go again. But Fletcher, quite properly, concluded that *Shoho* was sunk, and the rest of the ships with her were hardly worth the trouble. There was also the possibility that *Shoho* might not have been the only big ship sunk in the attack. When films of the strike were shown, viewers spotted an extraordinary sight. "Hold on a minute!" someone shouted. "Back up there!" The projector was put in reverse and rerun at a slower speed. The frames showed the bow of a Japanese heavy cruiser underwater. The pilots looked around at one another questioningly. Who had hit her?

"Finally," according to Admiral Fletcher, "one young fellow owned up to it. I sent for him, to offer my congratulations. When he got to the flag bridge, he was very apologetic. He explained that he had not reported the hit because he was afraid he might be court-martialed for not having followed the rest of the bombers. As he said, he had seen that the carrier was sinking, so he decided to try for the cruiser."

The young pilot was Ensign Thomas Brown, a Bombing 5 replacement who had come aboard *Yorktown* only nine days earlier, at Tongatabu, and had hardly said a word to anyone since. He received a commendation for his act

---

* Three by Flatley's fighters, one by Neilsen, one by Bigelow, and one by Schindler. Dick Crommelin and Dick Wright, on stay-at-home combat patrol, had knocked down another Kawanishi.

and from that day forward was known to all Yorktowners as Cruiser Brown.

Fletcher, however, realized that the battle was far from over. *Shoho* had been eliminated, but *Zuikaku* and *Shokaku,* the equals of *Yorktown* and *Lexington,* were still on the prowl. Too, Admiral Crace had not, as Fletcher had hoped, been able to destroy the invasion convoy. Crace, in fact, had had a bad time of it. As he had approached Jomard Passage, the Japanese had jumped him with three waves of land-based aircraft. His ships had shot down four of the enemy aircraft and somehow managed to evade all of their attackers' bombs and torpedoes. One of Crace's destroyers, U.S.S. *Farragut,* had even been forced to dodge bombs dropped by three eager American B-17s. When news that the invasion convoy had been turned back finally reached Crace, he headed for Australia.

Yorktown and *Lexington* pilots managed to get a bit of rest in the afternoon of May 7; but toward evening the weather started to clear, and *Yorktown* began picking up enemy aircraft on radar. The first report came at 5:47: enemy planes to the west, eighteen miles distant. *Lexington's* fighters were away first; they confirmed that the planes were the enemy's and engaged them. *Yorktown* fighters were also scrambled. The Japanese planes had been launched on the specific orders of Vice Admiral Takeo Takagi, commander of the carrier striking force. Rear Admiral Hara, commander of *Zuikaku* and *Shokaku,* had chosen his most experienced night-fighting pilots. The Japanese strike was made up of twelve dive bombers and fifteen torpedo planes, led by Lieutenant Commander Kakuichi Takahashi.

It was Takahashi's idea to strike the American carriers just after sunset when, in the dusk, he hoped to have an advantage over the gunners aboard *Yorktown* and *Lexington*. But the weather, as the Japanese planes approached from the east, remained sloppy, and Takahashi had just decided to abandon the attack when he was ambushed by *Lexington's* fighters. Soon after that, seven Wildcats from *Yorktown* joined the fight. The duel lasted fifty-two minutes, and *Yorktown* and *Lexington* pilots split evenly a total kill of eight enemy aircraft.

At about 6:55, *Yorktown* began recovering her Wildcats. A number were still up when, a few minutes after sunset, Lieutenant Norwood "Soupy" Campbell noticed that there appeared to be more planes circling over *Yorktown* than there should have been. Three of them swooped in from astern as though to catch *Yorktown's* arresting gear, then sheered away to starboard, and Campbell was certain that something was wrong. All American carriers had their bridges to starboard, and American pilots always turned to port to avoid the superstructure when they failed to hook the arresting cable. Certain Japanese carriers, however, were built with their superstructures on the port side, causing their pilots to sheer away to the starboard.

Yorktown's gunnery officer, Lieutenant Commander Ernie Davis, sized up the situation quickly. "Those aircraft in the landing pattern," he roared through the bullhorn, "are not friendly . . . repeat . . . not friendly." *Yorktown* fighters were ordered to pull out of the landing pattern; then Davis bawled an order that probably no American crew had heard in more than a century. "All hands," he said, "stand by to repel boarders!"

No one will ever know who fired the first shot, but it was not long in coming. Most of *Yorktown's* gun crews were already at battle stations, trying to get a little fresh air. One gun began firing; this triggered other itchy fingers. Seaman John Ginn was a loader on one of *Yorktown's* forward 1.1-inch mounts. "My gun jammed," he recalled later, "so I never got off one round in my first real battle action." Ginn was lucky, for he would never have to wonder whether he had helped shoot down Ensign Leslie Knox. The gunners also managed to shoot down one of the Japanese bombers.

After the threat of Japanese attack had subsided, the remainder of *Yorktown's* fighter flight was summoned back to the ship. But nervous gunners opened up again. The aircraft flown by Ensign Dick Enright was hit in the oil cooler; he landed safely. Ensign William Barnes got aboard with a bullet in his parachute pack and a wound in his lip.

Ensign John Baker became lost in the dark. For sixty-eight minutes, on orders from Captain Buckmaster, every available air officer, radarman, and radio operator stood by to help steer Baker home. Admiral Fletcher came into Air Plot to urge all hands to keep trying. Fletcher was a tough old surface ship sailor who had won a Medal of Honor at Vera Cruz in 1914, but he had a specially warm spot in his heart for young aviators.

By 8:28 P.M. the radar was no longer picking up Baker's plane. He was apparently a good distance away and at low altitude, putting him under the radar beam. Commander Pederson knew that Baker must be low on fuel. He spoke to Baker on radio, giving him a course and the distance to

Tagula Island. "My telephone talker was in tears," Pederson said afterward, "when I finally had to tell the pilot good-bye and good luck."

John Baker was lost. So was Knox, and *Lexington* lost a pilot who was also named Baker. The Japanese paid heavily for their deaths. Nine enemy planes went down near the American task force. Pilots of the other eighteen finally straightened out on course for their own carriers.* They were tired and short of gas. Only seven of the total of twenty-seven planes got home. A sixth of Admiral Takagi's air strength was gone, and it included some of the best pilots he had.

That night Admiral Fletcher and Captain Buckmaster considered a darting destroyer attack against the enemy strike force. Ensign John Lorenz, on late watch in *Yorktown's* bridge house, overheard the two American leaders drafting an actual attack message. Then Fletcher thought better of it. Admiral Takagi, remarkably enough, it is now known, was pursuing the same line of thought. He, too, decided against such an attack.

Aboard *Yorktown*, Lieutenant Jo-Jo Powers, a broken-nosed Irishman from New York who had been a boxing champion at the Naval Academy, rounded up the men of Bombing 5 and made a speech. The pilots and men listened respectfully, for Powers was something of a legend; he had served in the Asiatic Fleet before taking flight training. Each young Bombing 5 pilot, on first coming

---

* Earlier accounts, Morison's among them, suggest that the Japanese planes that came so close to *Yorktown* actually mistook *Yorktown* for one of their own carriers. This is improbable, for the pilots knew that their own ships were at least 100 miles away. A more credible explanation is that the Japanese planes, confused in the melee, joined up with some of the Wildcats, thinking that they were Japanese. Instead of being led home, they were led to *Yorktown*.

aboard *Yorktown,* had received an indoctrination course from Powers, who guided them over the entire ship, explaining how the guns worked, what the navigation procedures were, even arranging for them to stand bridge watches, an unusual duty for pilots. For some, it was the starting point of a career that led to the command of an aircraft carrier of their own.

Powers, that night, strode up and down as he spoke, his dark eyes burning. He recounted to them details of the strike on Tulagi and the attack on *Shoho.* He reminded Bombing 5 that there were still two Japanese carriers on the loose.

He concluded with these words: "Remember what they did to us at Pearl Harbor. The folks back home are counting on us. As for me, I'm going to get a hit on a Jap carrier tomorrow if I have to lay my bomb right on her flight deck." The men of Bombing 5 then turned in, little realizing that they would have reason to remember Powers' words all their lives.

Chapter Seven

★ ★ ★ ★ ★ ★ ★

★ ★ ★ The tropic moon rose at about 1 A.M. on May 8, bathing Task Force 17 in its soft glow. Fourteen ships—*Lexington, Yorktown*, five cruisers, and seven destroyers—were silhouetted like model ships on a painted ocean.

Yorktown and her escorts ran southeast, then turned west. Fletcher wanted to stay within striking distance of the invasion convoy, should it start for Port Moresby again. He knew that the two Japanese carriers (*Zuikaku* and *Shokaku*) were not far away, battered by the after-dark melee of the previous evening, but still deadly. Fletcher also knew the precise losses the Japanese had incurred through a message from the carriers to Rabaul that had been intercepted and decoded.

May 8 dawned clear over *Yorktown*, clouding Hubie Strange's weather outlook for the day. The weather front that had covered *Yorktown* on May 7 was now moving to the northeast, where the Japanese carriers were. The advantage that had been *Yorktown*'s the day before would now be shielding the Japanese.

At 6 A.M., *Shokaku* and *Zuikaku* launched a search group, fanning to the south and west. At 6:30, *Lexington* launched eighteen dive bombers, scanning in a full circle around the American task force.

Yorktown put up her combat air patrol of F4F fighters. She then launched eight dive bombers, each armed with a pair of depth charges. These planes were to guard against possible enemy submarine attack and, in the event of an enemy air attack, were under orders to jettison their depth charges and engage incoming torpedo planes.

With the planes up, Harry Bobbitt and five other mechanics of Scouting 5 assumed that they could grab a little sleep. They had been up all night with Chief Jake Ulmer, changing engines on two of the dive bombers; it had been a successful night's work, for both planes were now overhead on submarine patrol. Bobbitt, however, was so tired that he could not even make it belowdecks to his bunk. He crawled under a nearby 1.1-inch gun mount, put a life jacket under his head as a pillow, and fell into deep slumber.

The American task force zigzagged along a southeasterly course, awaiting word of a sighting. It came in at 8:20 A.M. A *Lexington* scout had spotted the Japanese. He remained on station, ducking in and out of clouds, amplifying his reports until Fletcher knew that there were two carriers, four cruisers, and many destroyers northeast of *Yorktown*, 175 miles away. At the same moment a Japanese scout was over Task Force 17. Radio interceptors heard him send his message, giving Admiral Takagi the precise location of the American fleet and the precise number of ships in it.

At 9 A.M., Admiral Takagi launched his strike—sixty-nine aircraft, including Zero fighters, Aichi-99 dive bombers, and Nakajima-97 torpedo planes, all again under the command of Lieutenant Commander Kakuichi Takahashi. At 8:48, twelve minutes earlier, Fletcher had ordered his strike—seventy-three aircraft, including Wildcat fighters, Dauntless dive bombers, and Devastator torpedo planes.

Never before had two opposing carrier forces launched such mighty attacks. The first great carrier battle was about to be joined, on almost precisely equal terms. The fate of New Guinea, perhaps of Australia, dangled precariously in the balance.

Fletcher, as he sent off his planes, radioed General Mac-Arthur in Australia, giving him his position and the Japanese position, hoping, of course, for help from the Army's B-17s, but hardly counting on it.

As the two strikes, the Americans heading northeast and the Japanese heading southwest, sped toward their targets, an almost ludicrous event occurred: they passed each other, in clear view of each other. Bill Fenton, leading six Wildcats from *Yorktown*, saw a group of planes off to his right. "They were too far away for us to identify," Fenton recalled later, "and we really didn't have enough spare fuel to go over and investigate them, so we merely waved at them and continued on our way."

By 10:32 A.M. the first of *Yorktown*'s planes were over *Shokaku* and *Zuikaku*; they could see the great enemy carriers occasionally through breaks in the heavy cloud cover. Lieutenant Commander Joe Taylor, desperately trying to get into battle with his lumbering torpedo planes, radioed to Bill Burch and his faster dive bombers, "Wait for me! Wait for me!"

Burch could not afford to wait very long, for every

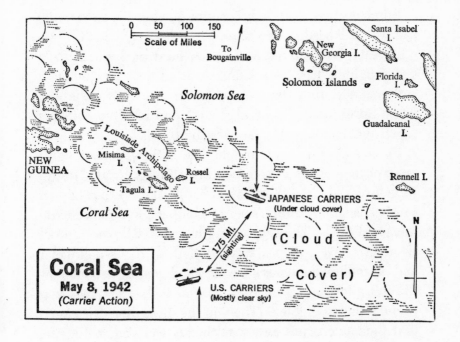

second he delayed gave the Japanese more time to launch fighter cover. Still, the dive bombers did have an opportunity to orbit for a few minutes in order to assemble in proper order. It was this brief delay that allowed *Zuikaku* to slide under a nearby rainsquall; she was not seen again for some time.

Burch decided that he had better go after *Shokaku* while she was still visible. He nosed over from 17,000 feet, six other dive bombers of Scouting 5 hard on his tail. Two dozen fighters had been launched to protect the Japanese carriers, and they had clawed their way into the sky while Burch was orbiting. As Burch and his dive bombers nosed over to attack, the Japanese hit them.

Burch's planes had a rough time of it. Japanese fighters swarmed around them like bees. Ensign J. H. "Jorgy" Jorgenson's landing gear was so badly shot up that he had to ditch later. Of Burch's seven bombers, five took hits in their fuel tanks. The self-sealing liners saved every one of them. All seven planes were dotted with 7.7-millimeter and 20-millimeter holes in wings and fuselage. Somehow Burch's pilots and gunners managed to knock down four of the Japanese fighters. Then, in the dive, they discovered that their telescopes and windshields were again fogging up. The day before, in the attack on *Shoho*, they had not had that problem, possibly because it had been made in clear, sunny weather. It was no wonder that Burch's bombers failed to score any hits.

Bombing 5 , led by Lieutenant Wally Short, had come in immediately behind Burch's Scouting 5. Short found that he was too close to *Shokaku* to dive, for he might overshoot, so he took his planes around in a 360-degree circle, fighting off Zeros part of the way. When his bombers finally made their attack, they had relatively little opposition because most of the Japanese fighters had peeled off and were attacking Burch's bombers.

Bill Guest, Ben Preston, and Hank McDowell, the last three of Short's pilots to make the bombing run, saw one of the most dramatic sights of the war:

Far below, through the clouds and the gunsmoke, they could see the dive bomber piloted by Jo-Jo Powers. It was staggering in its line of flight, taking hit after hit. Both Powers and his radioman, Everett Hill, were wounded, other pilots knew, because Powers had reported his condition by radio. They watched as Powers manhandled his bomber back on course. His plane was now in flames, and he was not much more than 200 feet above *Shokaku* when he dropped his 1,000-pound bomb. It crashed into *Shokaku's* flight deck only a second or two before Powers' bomber plunged into the ocean. Powers had kept his promise of the night before and died in doing it. He was awarded the Medal of Honor posthumously; anything less would have been unthinkable.

Yorktown's planes dropped twenty-three half-ton bombs over *Shokaku*. Besides the one dropped by Powers, only one other struck home. Those two hits were devastating. Fires broke out on the carrier almost immediately, and the forward end of her flight deck buckled so badly that she was finished, certainly for this battle. *Zuikaku* would have to recover her planes. Scouting 5 and Bombing 5 had done all they could—two bomb hits and nine enemy fighters downed.

Now it was Torpedo 5's turn. That this squadron got into

battle at all was something of a wonder. Before taking off from *Yorktown,* the pilots were told that they would have no fighter escort most of the way. Enlisted pilot Ed Williamson listened attentively and was shocked when he heard that lumbering Devastators were to proceed to their targets at an altitude of 5,000 feet. When the briefing was over, Williamson explained to Lieutenant Commander Joe Taylor that enemy planes could jump the vulnerable torpedo planes at that height, diving past them and coming up under their unprotected bellies. Williamson and Taylor agreed that Torpedo 5's twelve planes should hug the ocean surface after takeoff, just high enough so that their slipstreams wouldn't leave telltale wakes for high-flying enemy aircraft to see and low enough so that Zeros could not get under them.

Their low altitude took them right under the Japanese strike force. When Joe Taylor saw the enemy airplanes passing them far overhead, he blew Ed Williamson a kiss.

As the torpedo planes came within sight of the Japanese carriers, the Zeros were so busy battling dive bombers that they scarcely noticed the new wave of attackers. Taylor's planes managed, in fact, to go in with opposition from only two Japanese fighters, and this pair was shot down by Wildcat pilots Bill Woollen and John Adams. Yet even under these favorable conditions the torpedo planes had no luck. Again the torpedoes ran wild or bounced harmlessly off their target. Some of the torpedoes ran so slowly that *Shokaku* was able simply to turn away from them.

On the way back to their carrier, *Yorktown* planes accounted for three more enemy planes. Woollen and Adams teamed together again to knock down a Japanese torpedo bomber that was returning from the attack on *Yorktown*. Two other *Yorktown* pilots downed two Japanese bombers. *Yorktown*'s total kill was fifteen Japanese combat planes, plus another Kawanishi flying boat, caught by the stay-at-home combat air patrol.

Lexington's aircraft came in behind *Yorktown*'s and had almost no luck. Shortly after takeoff, one Torpedo 2 plane fell out of formation with engine trouble and had to turn back. Three Wildcats from Fighting 2 got lost and had to return before they ran out of gas. Then, as the weather grew worse, all the dive bombers in Scouting 2 got lost and had to turn back. Of the thirty-six planes launched against *Shokaku*, only twenty-one found her. They scored one bomb hit on her, at a cost of three Wildcats and three Dauntless dive bombers.

By noon all but two of *Yorktown*'s planes (never to return were Jo-Jo Powers and Ensign D. E. Chaffee) were heading home. A surprise awaited them, for the enemy strike they had passed had done against *Yorktown* as well as and probably better than they had done against *Shokaku*.

At about 10 A.M., Storekeeper Bob Milholin, one of the special operators trained by Vane Bennett, had the scope watch in *Yorktown*'s radar room. He was about to be relieved by Bennett when he said, "Hey, look at that!"

"It was one heck of a pip," Bennett later recalled. "It covered about an inch of our five-inch scope, so I knew it meant an awful lot of planes, spread out deep."

Milholin will never forget what he saw in that primitive radarscope. "For me," he said, "that sighting was the high point of the war. I remember that when word was passed to the crew that radar had picked up the Japanese planes while they were still sixty-eight miles away, they knew they had time to get ready for them, and they sent up a great big cheer for us."

Here, for the first time in the war, Americans really began to appreciate the tremendous advantage that their radar monopoly gave them in the Pacific. Task Force 17, thanks to Milholin's radar sighting, was able to calculate precisely when and from which direction the Japanese attack would come.

Control of all aircraft protecting Task Force 17 had been assigned to *Lexington's* fighter-director officer. He ordered more planes aloft, and four Wildcats from *Yorktown* responded; they were piloted by Jimmy Flatley, Brainard Macomber, Dick Crommelin, and Ed Bassett. *Lexington,* when the attack began, had twenty-five planes in the air; *Yorktown* had sixteen. They would not be nearly enough.

Later in the war, fighter interceptors aplenty would be stacked in layers, high and far out from their carriers, to meet and beat off an enemy attack. No such defense was arranged on May 8. Flatley's fighters, like Lieutenant Vince McCormack's, were sent out only 20 miles, stationed at 6,000 feet.

Flatley's flight, when it reached its station, found nothing but empty air. What Flatley did not know was that the Japanese attack force had already flown thousands of feet over his head. When he radioed *Yorktown* for instructions, he was told to return to the task force and take station directly above it. He and the three other pilots had barely climbed to 9,000 feet, to start home, when they ran

into a score or more of Japanese dive bombers and torpedo planes, all preparing to attack. He also noticed Zeros
hammering away at the dive bombers that *Yorktown* had
assigned to submarine patrol below him.

Flatley nosed over and began attacking the Japanese
planes. He shot down a Zero and drove several other planes
away. Dick Crommelin followed him down to 6,000 feet;
tangled with a Zero; leveled off in a fight with a second
Zero; and, finding himself at 3,000 feet, began climbing.
He was soon on the tail of a third Zero. He fired a burst,
and it rolled into a smoking dive and plunged into the
ocean. As Crommelin watched his Zero go down, he found
himself close to another one. Kicking rudder and dropping a wing, he went after it and sent it spinning toward
the ocean. A fifth Zero suddenly appeared right on Crommelin's tail. He shoved his Wildcat into a dive, building up
speed to run away. As he pulled out of the dive, he found
himself in the middle of a group of Zeros. He fired at every
plane that flicked across his gunsight, while the enemy
planes maneuvered desperately to get into attack position.
He managed an escape but ran into still another Zero as
he began to climb. Again he had to dive to escape.

As he pulled out of his dive, the only planes he could
see were Wildcats, but a stream of oil was coming out of
his wing. Bullets from one of the Zeros had cut the oil line
to his engine cooler. Crommelin throttled back and headed
for *Lexington,* the nearer of the two carriers; but his engine died short of his target, and he had to ditch. A destroyer picked him up.

Two other *Yorktown* fighter pilots, Art Brassfield and
Ed Mattson, joined the battle just as Flatley's group began

its attack. Brassfield and Mattson piled in, only to find two Zeros on their tails. Brassfield threw his Wildcat into a wild skid, and the Zero shot past him. He shot it down. Seconds later he spotted a Japanese dive bomber below him. He shot it down, too. Pulling out of his dive, he found three Zeros still with him. One round of 7.7 millimeter smashed into his cockpit clock, showering him with broken glass. Another round grazed his left leg. He escaped by flying into a cloud. Mattson went after three Zeros and, each time he opposed one, found another on his tail. He damaged one Zero but had his tail section badly shot up.

Thousands of feet below the fighter action, Lieutenant Roger Woodhull, leader of the eight dive bombers deployed to protect *Yorktown* from torpedo plane attack, was having his own troubles. Using dive bombers for anti-torpedo-plane work was a makeshift arrangement at best. A number of aviators, including Lieutenant Commander Oscar Pederson, had long argued that American carriers needed more fighter aircraft if bomber and torpedo strikes against the Japanese and the carriers themselves were to have adequate protection. As things stood, there simply were not enough fighters to do either job properly, when both had to be done simultaneously. The need for additional fighters would be only one of the many hard lessons of the Coral Sea.

Dive bombers had been assigned to anti-torpedo-plane work on the assumption that Japanese torpedo planes would be at least as slow and as vulnerable as the American Devastator was. Task Force 17 assumed that the Japanese would lumber in, just above the surface, making the same maximum 100 knots the armed Devastators were capable of. Thus, the American dive bombers, slow as they were, being free of a bombload, should be able to cope with that kind of enemy plane in such an attack.

That day at the Coral Sea Americans learned another lesson the hard way. The Japanese Nakajima-97 ship-based bomber was a highly versatile airplane. It could perform either high-level bombing or low-level torpedo missions. And it had approximately twice the speed of the Devastator.

Woodhull and his dive bomber pilots could only watch in amazement as the eighteen Japanese torpedo bombers raced toward *Yorktown* at 180 knots, 5,000 feet above the water. They roared over and past Woodhull's dive bombers, then nosed into steep power glides, leveling off at altitudes of 100 to 500 feet.

Observers on the two American carriers were also stunned. What kinds of planes were these to go so fast while lugging a torpedo? And what kinds of torpedoes were they carrying to survive such a long fall, then to level off and straighten out at proper depth on an attack course?

Each of the eighteen Japanese torpedo planes flew into attack position and began its launching approach without interference from a single American plane. Their escorting fighters, no longer needed for protection, turned on Woodhull's eight dive bombers. It was then the Japanese's turn for a surprise; the dive bombers had rear gunners, every one of whom appeared to be a sharpshooter. Woodhull's planes got off 2,800 rounds and shot down four Japanese fighters. But only half the dive bombers got home safely. Four *Yorktown* pilots, with their gunners, went down; none was recovered.

In less than twenty-four hours *Yorktown*'s aircraft had accounted for thirty Japanese carrier planes, at a cost to themselves of seven dive bombers and three fighters. The rest was now up to the carrier's ship's company.

Word of Milholin's radar sighting had been passed through *Yorktown* before 11 A.M. Captain Buckmaster estimated that the attack would come at about 11:15. Long before then, all hands—even Lieutenant Commander Ralph Arnold, the supply officer—were at battle stations. Arnold had talked Ernie Davis into letting him have command of a pair of .50-caliber machine guns on the bow.

On *Yorktown*'s flag bridge Admiral Fletcher turned to an aide. "Well," the admiral said, "we've done all we can. I guess the only thing left to do is put on this tin hat." The defense of *Yorktown*, in keeping with ancient naval custom, was now out of his hands. From this point on, it was the captain's show. Elliott Buckmaster, Brooklyn-born sailor-aviator, was in charge.

Ernie Davis' voice came booming over the loudspeaker: "Air department take cover. Gunnery department take over." At 11:06 A.M., Bennett and Milholin, watching the radarscope, reported that the Japanese were twenty miles away. Five minutes later, *Yorktown* lookouts could see the Japanese torpedo planes through their binoculars, range fifteen miles. Lieutenant Commander Delaney's sweating engineers wound up *Yorktown*'s four giant propellers until the great ship was knifing through the water at thirty knots.

Both *Yorktown* and *Lexington* were running southeast,

with *Yorktown* the farther south of the two ships. Because
she could accelerate faster than the larger *Lexington*, she
was able to draw ahead.

Along *Yorktown*'s catwalks, gunners began removing
from the muzzles of their .50s and .20s the covers used to
keep gun barrels free of salt spray. At 11:17 the torpedo
planes began turning in toward *Lexington*. A minute later,
other enemy planes headed for *Yorktown*.

Seaman Lew Godfrey, stationed in the radio direction
finder room, peeked through a port at the incoming Japanese planes and was astonished at what he saw. Some
weeks earlier Godfrey and other radiomen had been ordered to assemble certain classified documents. Among
them were tactical instructions for the pilots of Torpedo 5.
The Japanese torpedo planes, he now noted, were using
the same tactics recommended for Torpedo 5. The Japanese had formed a large arc; then they all had turned
simultaneously toward *Yorktown*. Godfrey assumed that
his ship was finished.

The heavy cruisers with *Yorktown* began firing their
eight-inch guns, aiming into the water at short range. The
explosions created towering waterspouts. Nello Tafi, a
plane captain in Scouting 5, reported that a cruiser "laid
her shells right in front of one Jap torpedo plane, and a big
column of water spouted up. The torpedo plane hit it
and did a complete somersault, landing in the water on its
back."

Quartermaster Howard Kiser, who was *Yorktown*'s best
helmsman, had the wheel watch when the attack began.
Kiser could steer "nothing to left or right" when so
ordered, and almost no one aboard could match his per-

formance. When the attack commenced, Kiser was inside *Yorktown's* armored wheelhouse, responding to orders from Captain Buckmaster. The captain could also have remained in the safety of the wheelhouse, peering out through slits in its armor plating, but he did not. "I felt it was imperative," he said after the battle, "that I have unobstructed visibility, to avoid torpedo and bombing attacks."

Buckmaster fought his battle from the open bridge, shouting wheel and engine orders to Kiser through the armor slits. His telephone talker, Seaman Nathan Ogdon, raced from side to side of *Yorktown's* island with the captain, and Chief Yeoman Henry Statchen, who was keeping a written record of the action, tried to keep up as best he could. Three other telephone talkers were on the bridge, all of them hard put to prevent the tangling of their lines.

Three planes came in from *Yorktown's* right rear, launching their torpedoes after they passed behind her stern. The torpedoes came in from rear left and were aimed for the carrier's port quarter. Buckmaster shouted an order through an armor slit, and Quartermaster Kiser spun the wheel hard right. This energized the huge motors in *Yorktown's* steering engine room, some 400 feet away. A giant piston retracted, another extended, and a mammoth steering post pivoted, swinging the great blade of *Yorktown's* rudder to starboard. *Yorktown's* stern dug into the sea, and the carrier's stern swung to port as her bow came right. The torpedoes passed harmlessly behind her.

Four more Nakajimas dropped their torpedoes, followed by two others. Chief Milt Wester of Fighting 42 was on *Yorktown's* hangar deck, waiting to service his planes, when he saw a Japanese torpedo about twenty feet away to starboard, maintaining a course parallel to *Yorktown*'s.

Wester grabbed the nearest telephone talker and ordered him, "Tell the bridge about that fish!"

The message was relayed to Captain Buckmaster, who replied to his talker, "There's one on the port side, too."

Seaman Ed Cavanaugh, whose job ordinarily was to scoop ice cream in the dairy bar, was manning the aftermost .50-caliber machine gun on the port catwalk. His station was just below the landing signal officer's platform. As the battle began, Lieutenant Norwood Campbell, the LSO, jumped down to give him a hand. Campbell pointed out the targets while Cavanaugh let fly. But almost every time he opened up on an enemy plane, one of *Yorktown*'s 5-inch guns would knock down the target first. The after 5-inchers nailed four Japanese planes, and the forward mounts three more before Cavanaugh got in a decent shot. A Nakajima somehow managed to get through the 5-inch gunfire and flew straight into Cavanaugh's sights. "I put a very long burst into him," Cavanaugh reported, "and he veered toward *Lexington*." The plane went into a sudden double snap roll and splashed into the water at *Lexington*'s side.

Answering Buckmaster's commands, *Yorktown* veered sharply from side to side. Nine torpedoes were fired at her, and he managed to evade them all. His gunners shot down eight of the nine torpedo planes.*

* *Lexington* was less fortunate. Japanese planes attacked her just one minute before the assault began on *Yorktown*. *Lexington* worked up to thirty knots quickly, using the tremendous power plant with which she had supplied electricity to the city of Tacoma, Washington, during a blackout a dozen years earlier. At sea she answered her helm sluggishly, well enough perhaps for a

At 11:24 A.M., the torpedo planes having completed their runs, Japanese dive bombers were in their attack. Buckmaster, still running *Yorktown* from the open bridge, watched the bombs start to fall, calling his orders to the helmsman through the slits of the armored wheelhouse. Somehow the ship—maneuvering like a destroyer—was able to dodge all the bombs. In the early moments of the battle Buckmaster had called Jack Delaney, the chief engineer, to order, "Give me everything you've got."

"You've got it, Captain!" Delaney had replied, for he had worked *Yorktown* up to 32.7 knots, or about 38 miles an hour. She was moving at destroyer speed, traveling so fast, in fact, that her escorting cruisers and destroyers, spread around her in Cruising Disposition Victor, could scarcely keep pace.

Bombs were falling all over the area. Seaman John Ginn, loading one of the rapid-fire 1.1-inch gun mounts, happened to glance up from his work. "What I saw froze me," he recalled later. "A Jap pilot let his bomb go, and it looked like it was coming right at me. My hesitation made me jam the barrel. A gunner's mate kept pounding on my foot and shouting at me to clear the gun, but it seemed a long time before he got through to me. I snapped out of it and cleared the barrel just as the bomb passed over my head. It exploded right below us, in the water."

Ginn's problem with jamming was not unusual. After the battle, gunnery officers calculated that there had been

---

battle cruiser, which she was originally built to be, but not nearly quickly enough for the carrier she had become. She managed to make one turn to starboard and one to port and was just coming right again when two torpedoes and four bombs slammed into her. Four more bombs, though near-misses, were damaging anyway. *Lexington* was hurt; at the time no one knew how badly.

more than fifty breakdowns or stoppages in the ship's sixteen rapid-fire 1.1-inch guns.

Marine Corporal Emil Matkowski had a similar scare. He was firing across the flight deck when his target released its 1,000-pound bomb. It headed straight for Matkowski, passing so close that the corporal swore he could have struck a match on it. The bomb severed a strand of a catwalk lifeline, a foot from where Matkowski was stationed, before it plunged into the ocean.

When they exploded in the water, the bombs threw spray—and steel fragments—across *Yorktown's* decks. At least a dozen Yorktowners were pinked by this form of waterborne shrapnel.

By 11:24 *Yorktown* gunners had knocked down four of the dive bombers (bringing the ship's total kill to forty-four Japanese planes) and had evaded nine torpedoes and ten half-ton bombs.

Then a Japanese pilot scored a hit.

Chapter Eight

★ ★ ★ ★ ★ ★ ★

★ ★ ★ Radioman Marlin Brock felt an odd thump orig-
inating not far from where he was stationed; then he heard
an excited voice in his headphones: "Bomb hit! Aft the
stack! Just forward of Number Two elevator!"

Captain Buckmaster had seen the plane approaching
and had watched its bomb as it was released. "Our antiaircraft fire cut the plane in two," he reported, "and parts
of the plane fell on each side of the ship." But the bomb
had been released seconds before the plane, an Aichi-
99, disintegrated.

Every Navy warship is divided into major sections and
is further divided into numbered and lettered sub-
compartments. *Yorktown* was divided into four major sections—A, B, C, and D—working from the bow aft. The
Japanese bomb plunged into the starboard side of *Yorktown*'s flight deck, near the beginning point of Section C,
between her center line and bridge superstructure.

Experts later concluded that the bomb was a twelve-
inch armor-piercing naval shell, fitted with fins, of the same
type that the Japanese had used at Pearl Harbor. It was
designed to reach a ship's vitals before detonating, and

that was precisely what happened. The bomb left a hole only one foot in diameter where it had penetrated *Yorktown*'s flight deck.

The bomb plunged through *Yorktown*'s flight deck and went into Bombing 5's ready room, where her pilots were briefed before combat. With most of her aircraft aloft, the room was nearly deserted. Budd Beistel, an aviation mechanic, was alone in the ready room, manning a telephone headset. He watched in fascination as the bomb plunged into his compartment, struck a steel safe, then glanced inboard and downward. Beistel pushed the button on his phone and hesitatingly informed the bridge, "Sir, I think a bomb just passed through here!"

Below the ready room was the hangar deck. On duty there was a group of men called Repair 7. It was composed, like all repair groups, of an odd assortment of sailors. Some of them were musicians and yeomen; others were highly skilled electricians, shipfitters, carpenters, and machinist's mates. Their job was to repair any damage inflicted by the enemy, minutes after it occurred.

Seaman Emil Puksar, one of the members of Repair 7, later reported, "That bomb came through the overhead and went into the deck about four feet from me." But before it plunged farther into *Yorktown*'s vital regions, it took away half of Seaman Pat Palumbo's skull. Palumbo was the first member of *Yorktown*'s ship's company, as the men not in a carrier's air group are called, to die as the result of enemy action.

Certain members of Repair 7, curious to see what had happened after the bomb had torn through the hangar deck, ran to the hole the bomb had made and peered through it. The uprushing explosion killed Seaman Walter Krupinski, injured Fred Symonis, and cost Ed Pettipas an eye. Aviation Mechanic Bill Josen, who had gone nowhere near the hole, was killed by shrapnel that came out of it. The same shrapnel pierced the wallet in the rear pocket of Chief Art Powers and pinked him in a sensitive area of his body.

An aircraft carrier's hangar deck is also its main, or first, deck. Below, other decks are numbered in sequence, all the way down to the ship's double bottom. In the Japanese bomb's path, below the hangar deck, were the Marine Corps berthing compartment, which was on the second deck; the ship's store compartment on the third deck; and an aviation spare parts storeroom on the fourth deck. Below the fourth deck, made of solid armor plating, was *Yorktown*'s main engine room.

The bomb pierced the flight deck, ready room, hangar deck, Marines' compartment, and ship's store compartment. It finally detonated when it struck the armor plate in the aviation storeroom. It exploded, in fact, almost directly over Commander Delaney's head.

The explosion gutted the aviation storeroom on the fourth deck; fortunately, no one was in it at the time. On the second deck it wrecked lockers and rifles in the Marines' compartment, which was also deserted. On the third deck, in the ship's store compartment, a large one, running almost the full width of the ship, fifty-four men, members of Repair 5, were on duty.

The bomb, bursting on the deck below, ripped up through this compartment and killed the men of Repair 5,

Admiral Frank Jack Fletcher, commander of American aircraft carrier forces during the battles of the Coral Sea and Midway. *Below:* Elliott Buckmaster, Commanding Officer of U.S.S. *Yorktown* during the battles of the Coral Sea and Midway.

Yorktown on her christening day in 1936. She was commissioned the following year.

COURTESY OF W. S. WOOLLEN

Pilots of *Yorktown*'s Fighting 42. Left to right, front row: B. F. Macomber, A. J. Brassfield, R. M. Plott, W. N. Leonard, C. R. Fenton, O. Pederson, V. F. McCormack, W. S. Woollen, L. L. Knox. Rear row: E. Mattson, R. L. Wright, H. B. Gibbs, W. B. Barnes, J. D. Baker, E. S. McCuskey, R. Crommelin, J. P. Adams, E. Bassett, W. Haas. *Below,* pilots of Torpedo 3. Left to right, front row: C. Osberg, J. Baker, O. Powers, D. Roche, D. Weissenborn, W. Weis. Center row: R. Suesens, P. Hart, L. Massey, C. Howard, J. Myers, F. Herriman. Rear Row: H. Corl, W. Osmus, W. Snider, J. Armitage, G. Stablein, L. Smith, J. Haas, W. Esders.

COURTESY OF FRED HERRIMAN

Speeding Japanese carrier *Shoho* on fire in Battle of the Coral Sea after being struck by *Yorktown* pilots who reported that she "went right under, doing twenty-one knots." *Below*, U.S.S. *Lexington*, aflame and being abandoned after Japanese aerial attack in the Battle of the Coral Sea.

Commander Arnold True, skipper of the destroyer U.S.S. *Hammann*, sunk with *Yorktown* by Japanese submarine June 6, 1942. *Below,* Ed Williamson, *Yorktown* enlisted torpedo plane pilot who put a torpedo into Japanese carrier *Shoho* in Battle of the Coral Sea.

COURTESY OF M. F. LESLIE

Squadron Commander Max Leslie, who, although his own bomb had been accidentally jettisoned earlier, led Bombing 3 against the Japanese at Midway. His second-in-command of the squadron, Lieutenant "Swede" Holmberg, scored the first hit against the enemy in that battle.

Yorktown dive bomber "ditching" astern of cruiser U.S.S. *Astoria* during Battle of Midway. Plane was that of either Lieutenant Commander Max Leslie or Lieutenant "Swede" Holmberg, both of whom ran out of fuel following successful strike against enemy at Midway.

Japanese cruiser *Mogami*, following attack by Ensign Ben Preston and other *Yorktown* pilots after that carrier was put out of action in the Battle of Midway. Heavily damaged, *Mogami* limped back to Japan, where she was out of action for many months.

Yorktown, aflame after the first Japanese torpedo plane attack against her in Battle of Midway. She was promptly back in action, and when she was hit a second time, the Japanese erroneously reported that they had inflicted serious damage against another American carrier.

Crewman repairing hole in *Yorktown's* deck made by bomb in the first Japanese aerial attack at Midway. Blast killed nearly all of crew manning guns at left. A short time later the guns were back in action (*below*), manned by firemen and mess cooks brought from lower decks. Medical corpsmen work over survivor at right.

U.S.S. *Yorktown* at the precise moment when she was struck by aerial torpedoes released by Japanese bombers in the battle of Midway, June 4, 1942. Black clouds are from anti-aircraft guns fired by *Yorktown* and ships in her defensive screen.

Yorktown after she had been abandoned on June 4, 1942, following seemingly fatal penetration by two Japanese aerial torpedoes. Destroyer standing by is probably U.S.S. *Hughes,* left alone to guard the carrier against possible capture should she fail to sink as expected.

NAVY DEPARTMENT

Yorktown and her protective screen on morning of June 6, 1942. *Below*, destroyers on patrol around carrier. One of the screen was U.S.S. *Hammann*, broken in two and sunk immediately when Japanese submarine, approaching from carrier's high side, fired torpedoes to sink her finally as an American boarding party was working to right the ship.

NAVY DEPARTMENT

U.S.S. *Hammann*, one of destroyers protecting *Yorktown* on morning of June 6, 1942, going down with great loss of life two minutes after being struck by torpedo from Japanese submarine *I-168*. *Hammann* was lying close to *Yorktown* in order to supply electrical power to damage-repair crew working to correct carrier's dangerous list to port. It is believed that *Yorktown* could have been saved had daring submarine commander not interrupted repair operations.

Yorktown on her side following Japanese submarine torpedo attack, June 6, 1942. *Below*, gigantic hole blown in carrier's side can be seen to left of center.

U.S.S. *Yorktown*, heroine of the battles of the Coral Sea and Midway, takes the final plunge June 6, 1942, as her protective screen circles close by.

waiting there to repair damage occurring elsewhere in the ship. Forty-one of the men were killed instantly.

Machinist's Mate Worth Hare survived the explosion, although he was badly burned. He lost consciousness, came to, then led survivors to safety in the next compartment, aft, where Repair 4 was stationed.

Lieutenant Milton Ricketts, officer in charge of Repair 5, was knocked over a fireplug and his skull was smashed; yet he managed to pay out hose and turn on the water before he died, thereby probably saving a number of lives. He was posthumously awarded *Yorktown*'s second Medal of Honor for deeds done that day.

Parts of the exploding bomb pierced bulkheads fore and aft of the Repair 5 compartment. One piece caught Arthur Triplett, ship's baker, in the ribs. "I got to sick bay and sat down outside," Triplett reported, "figuring I could wait until the serious cases were treated. A corpsman came by, jabbed me with morphine, and gave me a shot of Ten High whiskey. Then he went off to tend other wounded." But before departing, the corpsman set the bottle of whiskey on the deck. "I figured I might as well be comfortable," Triplett said, "so I finished off the rest of the whiskey." He then dozed off. When he awoke, he staggered into *Yorktown*'s sick bay just as doctors were identifying a severed head as his. "Like hell it is!" Triplett roared in shock and indignation.

From start to finish, *Yorktown*'s battle lasted only thirteen minutes. By 11:31 A.M. the surviving Japanese planes had begun to head for their rendezvous point. When the skies appeared clear of the enemy, Buckmaster directed

his executive officer, Commander Dixie Kiefer, to go below and make a personal assessment of the battle damage.

A certain amount of damage was obvious from the
flight deck. One near-miss had rocked *Yorktown* so hard
that her radar antenna, towering 100 feet above her water-
line, had been damaged. Emergency repairs were quickly
made.

Belowdecks, concussion had damaged the exhaust uptakes from Fire Rooms 7, 8, and 9, *Yorktown*'s superheater
boilers. Because the uptakes could not carry smoke from
the boilers up through the carrier's stacks, it was forced
into the firerooms, making them untenable. Volunteers,
fighting through the smoke, cleared the uptakes. Even with
the uptakes not operating, *Yorktown* managed to maintain
a speed of twenty-four knots.

The most serious damage, Kiefer discovered, was on
Yorktown's port side, the result of two near-misses.
There bombs exploding in the water had acted like depth
charges, blasting open seams in the carrier's portside fuel
tanks, and the carrier's lifeblood was gushing through the
cracks. With the tanker *Neosho* sunk, there was no way of
knowing when *Yorktown* might get another refueling. If
she ran dry, she would be a helpless, floating hulk.

First, though, it was time to clean up the damage, carry
away the bodies, and collect the pieces. Musician Ed
Oakley supervised the removal of the dead from Repair 5
to the hangar deck. Corpsmen bribed sailors with shots of
Ten High to get the work done. Shipfitter Earl Fogarty
found the body of Bill Kowalcewski, a machinist's mate,
and the dead man's brother, Victor, a fireman, helped carry
the body topside.

Most of the crew skipped supper that night, content to eat the 10,000 candy bars passed around before the battle began. Those who did visit the galley wished that they had not, for the trip involved passing the sick bay and looking at a pile of severed arms and legs. Funeral services for *Yorktown*'s dead were held by Chaplain Frank Hamilton at midnight. Bodies were placed in white mattress covers, then weighted down with five-inch shells. Only a handful of Yorktowners could stomach the burial detail; most of those who did were pharmacist's mates. The bodies were slipped over the side, but even when that grisly job was done, Hospital Corpsman Vince Haley recalled, "We had a pile of spare human parts left over. There was nothing to do but put all of them into a sack and let it go."

At 12:31 P.M., while the wounded were being treated and the dead collected, *Yorktown* began recovering her attack group. One of the first planes aboard was Lieutenant Floyd Moan's dive bomber. Both the pilot and his radioman, Bob Hodgens, were wounded. The plane crashed into *Yorktown*'s island, a total wreck. It had been hit by twenty-two Japanese slugs. The crew was pulled out of the wreckage, and what was left of the plane was shoved over the side.

By 1 P.M. all of *Yorktown*'s planes that were to return had come home. Missing, never to be recovered, were seven dive bombers and one fighter. Dick Crommelin was aboard a destroyer; so were Ensign Jorgenson and his gunner, Tony Brunetti. Of the six other crews, only Lieutenant Rowley and Seaman Musgrove were still alive.

Twenty-two of the planes that *Yorktown* recovered were damaged, some with as many as twenty-six bullet and can-

non holes in their self-sealing fuel tanks. Of the twenty
tanks hit by gunfire, only three had leaked, and of those
three, two did not begin to leak until the planes were safely
back aboard the carrier.

The Japanese, on the other hand, had been reduced to
an effective aircraft force of only 9 bombers, 6 torpedo
planes, and 24 fighters. More than 100 Japanese planes,
including snoopers and those aboard *Shoho* when she went
down, had been destroyed. Perhaps even more serious for
Japan, their veteran pilots had been lost with them. Among
them was Lieutenant Commander Takahashi, leader of
the two strikes against the American carriers and the man
who had led the Japanese dive bombers against Pearl Harbor.

Still, the Japanese had succeeded better than they knew.
Lexington, hit by two torpedoes and four bombs, seemed
at first to be seaworthy enough. She slowed down briefly
following the attack, picked up speed again, and even
recovered some of her aircraft, a number of which were
refueled and launched again. Then, at 12:47, an immense
explosion shook the 27,000-ton ship. Her amidships elevator popped up above the flight deck and settled back
with a crazy bulge in it. *Lexington's* crew, like *Shokaku's,*
was forced to fight a series of fierce fires.

Even then, *Lexington* seemed to be holding her own. In
time she reported that all her fires had been put out. At
2:45 P.M. she was rocked by another major explosion; fires
again broke out all over her. This time there was no
quenching them. By 4:30 *Lexington* stopped dead in the
water. At 5:10 the crew began abandoning ship, destroyers and cruisers picking up 2,700 men. As darkness fell, the

old ship was a mass of flames. The destroyer *Phelps* was ordered to move in and sink her with torpedoes. She went down at 8 P.M. Feelings aboard *Yorktown* were mixed; the crew hated to see her go, but they had also been concerned by her flames, which had illuminated the ocean for miles around.

Yorktown took aboard nineteen orphan planes from *Lexington* and, by late afternoon, had repaired seventeen of them. Fletcher reasoned that he might need them, for he believed a Japanese task force was in hot pursuit. The next day, May 9, one of *Yorktown's* scouts did, in fact, report the sighting of an enemy aircraft carrier, 175 miles to the northwest. Fletcher launched all available dive bombers and even sent Commander Butch Schindler flying to Australia, to seek B-17 assistance from MacArthur. But when the American carrier strike, accompanied by fourteen B-17's, arrived over the target, the enemy carrier turned out to be Lihau Reef, a small rock outcropping northeast of Australia. From 20,000 feet it looked like a carrier task force, streaming a white wake behind it.

Yorktown had her planes back aboard by noon, except for Ensign Lawrence Traynor's dive bomber, which crashed over the side. Traynor and his radioman, Jim Cales, were picked up by the destroyer *Morris*.

Then *Yorktown's* radar went dead again. Back up the mast went Vane Bennett and Speedy Attaway to discover that explosions during the battle had loosened the clamp holding the antenna to the mast. The antenna, a bulky bedspring-like apparatus, had fallen over at a slant. Bennett, conferring with Buckmaster, worked out an ingenious plan to make repairs. The ship was turned downwind, matching her speed with that of the prevailing wind, so that the apparent wind across her flight deck was zero. With this artificial calm, Bennett, Attaway, Chief Electrician's Mate Frank Flynn, and a working party of eight climbed the mast and pushed the antenna upright again.

Bennett then instructed the working party to walk the antenna around and around, unscrewing it from its base. With that done, the antenna was tipped to one side while Attaway and Flynn reached inside the base to make repairs. Then the working party walked the antenna in the opposite direction, screwing it firmly into place. As these repairs were in progress, the men stationed at Ensign John Lorenz's after 1.1-inch gun mounts kept their eyes fastened on the radar antenna of the escort cruiser *Portland*. If that antenna stopped, it meant that a target had been picked up. Fortunately, *Portland*'s antenna continued to revolve without interruption.

Yorktown need not have worried, for the Japanese, just as punched out as the Americans, were also retreating. The Coral Sea was again quiet.

The first carrier-against-carrier battle was over. Was there a winner?

In terms of ships destroyed, the Japanese clearly had the edge. They had sunk *Lexington*, a great carrier. American pilots had destroyed *Shoho*, a third-rate carrier. Two destroyers had been destroyed: *Kikuzuki* by the Americans, *Sims* by the Japanese. The only other ship destroyed of any consequence was the American oiler *Neosho*.

The whole point of the battle had been Port Moresby; the Japanese had wanted to take it; the Americans had wanted to protect it from them. Port Moresby had been saved, and Australia at the very least had been given a respite. The Japanese had taken Tulagi; getting it back, along with Guadalcanal, would be a long, bloody, and sometimes uncertain business.

The Japanese were still preparing for a showdown naval battle at Midway, but when that battle came, the two front-line carriers from the Coral Sea, *Shokaku* and *Zuikaku*, would be absent, *Shokaku* because of battle damage and *Zuikaku* because of a shortage of planes and pilots. *Yorktown* had been chiefly responsible for this.

On May 10 the Navy Department issued a communiqué about the five-day battle, reporting that twenty-five Japanese ships had been definitely sunk, five probably sunk, and four possibly sunk. "Australia Saved!" headlines cried. The Japanese, in an equally absurd communiqué, reported that both American carriers, *Yorktown* and *Lexington*, had been sunk; they also reported they had destroyed several battleships, even though none had been there.

The next day, May 11, Fletcher divided his forces. He ordered cruisers *Astoria*, *New Orleans*, and *Minneapolis*, and four destroyers to put into Nouméa, New Caledonia. *Yorktown* and the other ships, carrying the crew members from *Lexington*, headed once again for Tongatabu. York-towners speculated that Fletcher did not want the carrier at Nouméa for fear that word of her damaged condition would slip out. New Caledonia was in Free French hands, but the place, it was said, also harbored Nazi sympathizers.

Far to the northeast of *Yorktown*, Admiral Nimitz was still worried, needlessly, about the security of Port

Moresby. One of his carriers in the southwest Pacific was sunk; the other was damaged. That left him only *Hornet* and *Enterprise*, operating out of Pearl Harbor. Although he suspected that the Japanese were preparing to start something at Midway, he rushed *Hornet* and *Enterprise* southwest, leaving a vulnerable flank unprotected.

Yorktown dropped anchor at Tongatabu on May 17, and no one was happier about it than Commander Delaney. He had used all of *Yorktown*'s fuel to get there and was burning diesel fuel as he pulled into Nukualofa Anchorage. The first order of business was refueling, and the only fuel available was in a British ship that had recently put into the harbor. "The stuff was lousy, loaded with sulfur or something," a *Yorktown* engineer recalled. Still, it would burn, and *Yorktown* and her escorts took all of it they could get.

An inspection of *Yorktown*'s fuel tank damage revealed that permanent repairs could be made only in dry dock. Yorktowners, with the nearest dry dock thousands of miles away, did the best they could.

As fuel was being taken aboard and as temporary repairs were being made, *Yorktown* remained on battle alert, for Fletcher was still not convinced that the enemy might not be near at hand. All the guns were manned, and Ensign John Lorenz was assigned to patrol the seventy-five-foot-wide entrance to the channel in a forty-foot motor launch. His crew was armed with Springfield rifles and several Browning submachine guns. One night, ludicrously, the coxswain managed to run the launch on some rocks, and the crew was marooned there for two hours.

On May 24, Fletcher, as commander of Task Force 17, received a high-priority top-secret message from the commander in chief of the U.S. Pacific fleet. "What it said," Fletcher recalled, "was simply this: Get the hell back here, quick."

Chapter Nine

★ ★ ★ ★ ★ ★ ★

★ ★ ★ Midway Atoll is a miserable handful of land. Surrounded on almost all sides by a barrier reef, it contains only two pieces of high ground—Sand Island, barely two miles long, and Eastern Island, hardly a mile long. In the center of the atoll is a lagoon, with a narrow ship's channel leading into it. On the atoll's western edge is an open harbor of sorts. Yet this atoll, this flyspeck of neglected real estate, became in late May, 1942, the object of the greatest naval confrontation the world had ever seen.

The capture of Port Moresby, thwarted (only temporarily, the Japanese thought) by the Battle of the Coral Sea, was a part of phase two of Japanese strategy. The same phase two dictated the capture of Midway and Kiska in the western Aleutians. Phase three, for which planning was already in its final stages, involved the capture of Samoa, Fiji, and New Caledonia.

The Japanese idea was to develop an outer perimeter, an inviolable defensive line, that no American force would ever be able to penetrate. The line, when phase three had been completed, would run from Kiska far in the north, south (and even a little east) to Midway, southwest to

Wake Island, the Marshalls, and the Gilberts; loop around Samoa, Fiji, and New Caledonia; and anchor finally at Port Moresby.

Part of the Japanese strategy—an essential part—was a showdown battle with the U.S. Pacific fleet.* A move against Midway, Admiral Yamamoto reasoned, would bring that fleet into action. The Americans, he thought correctly, would never allow Midway to fall, as earlier they had allowed Wake to fall. Midway, after all, was the far outpost of the Hawaiian Islands, little more than 1,000 miles from Pearl Harbor itself.

For the combined action against Midway and the Aleutians, the Japanese assembled almost everything they had except the carriers *Shokaku* and *Zuikaku,* the former having put into the Inland Sea for repairs and the latter being immobile at Truk, awaiting new planes and new pilots. The backbone of the Japanese force, as a result, was four big carriers, instead of six—*Akagi, Kaga, Hiryu,* and *Soryu,* carrying a total of 93 fighters, 86 bombers, and 93 torpedo planes, 272 aircraft in all. All four carriers had taken part in the attack on Pearl Harbor and were under command of Admiral Chuichi Nagumo. The assignment of the carrier force was to hunt down and destroy the U.S. Pacific fleet. Accompanying the carrier force were two battleships, two cruisers, and twelve destroyers.

There were, in addition, two occupation forces. The

* The "one decisive battle" objective was a key factor in both Japanese and American prewar naval strategy in the Pacific. Destroy the Japanese Navy, American officers reasoned, and the path was clear to Tokyo. Destroy the U.S. Pacific fleet, Japanese officers reasoned, and it would be years before their homeland could be threatened. This would allow time for making defenses so strong that America, stymied, might agree to a negotiated peace, with Japan gaining all her Asian objectives.

Midway force, transporting 5,000 soldiers, consisted of one small carrier, two battleships, eight cruisers, and ten destroyers. The Aleutians force consisted of two small carriers, six cruisers, and thirteen destroyers. It transported 500 soldiers and 700 labor troops.

The heavy Japanese surface ships were concentrated into a main body, which was to take up a position between Midway and the Aleutians. It consisted of seven battleships, a very small old carrier, two cruisers, and thirteen destroyers. It also included two ships loaded with midget submarines, which would be based ashore after Midway was taken, for its defense. The great Japanese Admiral Yamamoto was sailing in the main body, flying his flag from the immense 60,000-ton battleship *Yamato*.

The Japanese Navy, obviously, was spread widely over the Pacific Ocean. All postbattle critics have varying views on the advisability of this strategy. Admiral Morison, in *History of United States Naval Operations in World War II*, suggests that Yamamoto did not anticipate that the Americans would oppose him in the initial phases of the invasion of Midway. Thus, says Morison, Yamamoto would have time to consolidate his forces and crush the Americans.

Looking at plans from Yamamoto's viewpoint, however, things may be seen differently. Even without the main body, he had far more than sufficient strength to crush the American forces. So his battleship force was actually right where it ought to be, acting as a powerful roving linebacker, ready to rush in where needed. If the American fleet, as he hoped it would be, was lured toward the

Aleutians, the main body could combine with other forces there to sink it. If it moved on Midway, that would be the main body's line of march. And it could be used in either place as a mop-up force.

Admiral Chester Nimitz, at Pearl Harbor, counted up what he had to oppose this mighty armada. It was not much. Task Force 17, again, would be commanded by Admiral Fletcher in *Yorktown,* but with *Lexington* gone, *Yorktown* was the only carrier in the task force. With *Yorktown* would be two cruisers and six destroyers. One of those destroyers would again be *Hammann.* Task Force 16, under the command of Rear Admiral Raymond A. Spruance (Halsey had been hospitalized with a skin disease), consisted of the carriers *Enterprise* and *Hornet,* six cruisers, and nine destroyers.

Both sides also had a number of submarines. The Japanese had ordered two submarine squadrons to take up picket-line duty north of Hawaii, but the boats in both squadrons were old and slow; submarine officers pleaded with members of Yamamoto's staff to substitute faster, fresher boats in their place. The plea was turned down. The result was that by the time the Japanese submarines arrived on station, the three American carriers had already slipped through their net.

One submarine, not part of the net, was *I-168,* commanded by Lieutenant Commander Yahachi Tanabe, who had orders to scout close to Midway. By May 31 she was on station, ready for action. *I-168* was to play a vital part in *Yorktown's* fate.

Yorktown, the ship that almost alone had reduced the

odds in the approaching battle from impossible to merely overwhelming, hoisted anchor at Tongatabu on May 24 and began steaming for Pearl Harbor. May 26 was a day to note; it marked *Yorktown's* hundredth day at sea without proper replenishment, a record no other modern major American warship had even approached.

That evening, before the movie on the hangar deck began, *Yorktown's* band broke its instruments out of a month's storage and gave the crew a concert. Special guests, seated front and center, were the burned and blackened survivors of Repair 5.

Movie time aboard a Navy ship is attended by an unchanging protocol when the commanding officer is aboard. The captain waits until just before showtime to make his appearance. He is preceded by a master-at-arms who roars, "Attention on deck!" All officers and men then rise to respectful attention until the captain is seated and the master-at-arms thunders, "Seats!" Seconds later the film starts rolling.

On the night of May 26 the sailors of *Yorktown* did not merely rise respectfully when Captain Elliott Buckmaster made his appearance. They leaped to their feet, plunging into a frenzy of cheering, stamping, whistling, and shouting. It was an ovation to the man who had steered them through the Coral Sea and might now have to steer them through they knew not what. For all that she had been through, there was still plenty of spirit in bedraggled Old Yorky.

Japanese sailors, too, were cheering that night, for it was their Navy Day, the thirty-seventh anniversary of Ad-

miral Heihachiro Togo's annihilation of a Russian fleet at
the Battle of Tsushima.*

On May 27, *Yorktown* steamed up Pearl Harbor's narrow channel to the accompaniment of whistles, sirens, and
cheers, circled Ford Island, and headed straight into dry
dock. Water was drained from the basin until *Yorktown*
was resting on keel blocks; more water was drained away
until the torn plates from which her oil had been gushing
were fully exposed. Admiral Nimitz came aboard to inspect damage personally. Then the carrier was turned over
to the yard's workmen.

To this day, the story has persisted that 1,400 shipyard
workmen fully repaired *Yorktown* in three days and three
nights. Admiral Morison, for one, implies that *Yorktown's*
"structural strength," including her bulkhead stanchions,
was adequately restored. These workmen were chiefly a
supply and reprovisioning force. It is far from accurate to
presume that the repairs were anything but very rough,
what sailors call jury rig. Welders did, in fact, patch *Yorktown's* hull, and damaged compartments were braced with
timbers. But only a few of the sprung watertight doors
were fixed, and Commander Delaney's three superheater
boilers, knocked out at the Coral Sea, were not even
touched. *Yorktown* would never be able to top twenty-
seven knots, her engineers decided.

* For the Japanese, however, it was May 27, not May 26, because the
Japanese Navy used the East Longitude date and set their clocks on Tokyo
time. This sort of thing makes researching the Battle of Midway a nightmare.
Japanese log entries are twenty-one hours later than Midway time. Task Forces
16 and 17 used the same West Longitude date as Midway, but their time of day
was Zone plus ten, two hours later than Midway's. In the account that
follows, all times, for both sides, are those used at Midway.

Yorktowners hoped, understandably enough, that their ship would be ordered back to the West Coast, where they would get liberty and rest. Seaman Warren Woodard was one of the many hopeful crew members, but he began to have his doubts as he watched a big crane lift the undersized railroad cars of the Oahu Railway Company to the flight deck for unloading. *Yorktown,* Woodard suddenly decided, was taking on far too much in the way of stores for a trip to a Stateside yard. The one man elated by *Yorktown's* provisioning was Chief Commissary Steward Cal Callaway. Wherever *Yorktown* was going, the crew was going to eat well; Callaway signed delivery orders for seventy-five days' worth of provisions.

Not all these provisions reached *Yorktown's* food lockers. Seaman Emil Puksar, recalling the old maritime adage "One hand for yourself, one hand for the ship" managed to make off with a canned ham and several gallon cans of peaches, pineapples, and pears while he was working with a provisioning party. Ship's Cook Tomas Saxon, one of the few Yorktowners allowed liberty ashore, smuggled a rabbit aboard. No one was sure whether it was a pet or the makings of a stew.

As *Yorktown* had approached Pearl Harbor, all her planes that would fly had been sent ashore. A few days later disturbing news came back from shore headquarters: some of the aircraft would not be coming back.

Torpedo 5, with the important exception of her pilots, radiomen, and bombardiers, would remain aboard. The airmen would be replaced by Torpedo 3, a *Saratoga* squadron that had been put ashore months before when their carrier had limped off to Bremerton shipyard in the state of Washington with a torpedo hole in her side. *Yorktown's* torpedo airmen were under orders to start checking out in the new Grumman TBF Avengers with which the carrier was being provided.

Bombing 5 was to come back aboard following the completion of repairs, but this time it would be acting as *Yorktown's* scout squadron, assuming, temporarily, the designation Scouting 5. The old Scouting 5, which had taken a very bad beating at the Coral Sea, would remain ashore, to be replaced by another *Saratoga* squadron, Bombing 3. Last, Fighting 42's name would be changed to Fighting 3, with a new skipper and a new executive officer. Even so, sixteen of its pilots would be *Yorktown* veterans.

The fighting squadron's strength was being increased, and that was good news. Apparently someone had finally listened to complaints and suggestions from frontline aviators. This time out, *Yorktown* would carry twenty-seven Wildcats, instead of only eighteen.

On balance, however, Yorktowners were upset. Commandar Oscar Pederson, air group commander, was furious. No good coach, he argued, ever broke up a winning team, and *Yorktown's* old team had seen more combat than any other air group in the Navy. Pederson even went ashore to complain to Rear Admiral Leigh Noyes, commander of the Navy's Pacific air arm. It did no good; the orders stood as written.

Ten days earlier, Pederson had written a prophetic note in his account of the Coral Sea action, in which he recorded that the Japanese escort ships scattered during attacks instead of closing in around their carriers. "In the event that the Japanese change their system and put

a heavy cordon of ships around their large vessels," Pederson wrote, "it is doubtful whether a successful torpedo attack could be launched by TBDs without loss of the major
part of the squadron."

Yorktown would have to go into her final battle with the
obsolescent Devastator torpedo planes. At least, however,
she was getting a better version of the Wildcat fighter
plane, the F4F-4.

Assigned as chief engineering officer for Fighting 3, né
Fighting 42, was Chief Milt Wester. When he heard that
Yorktown was going to get F4F-4s in place of F4F-3s, he
began itching to inspect the new version, for after all, it
would be his job to tend the planes. But in a typically in-
furiating example of bureaucratic red tape, he was not allowed to go ashore to look at the new aircraft. "I was really
in trouble," Wester stated. "These were new-type aircraft,
which we knew nothing about, and I couldn't go ashore to
get a little indoctrination because the word had been
passed that no one was to leave the ship."

On May 28, *Hornet* and *Enterprise* steamed out of Pearl
Harbor. A number of Yorktowners, watching them depart, still labored under the impression that those two carriers would fight the next battle while *Yorktown* headed
Stateside for overhaul and repair. At 9 A.M. on May 30 the
dry dock was reflooded and *Yorktown* eased out of it,
under way again, thereby maintaining her reputation as
a steamer. Since January 1, 1941, she had logged more
than 450 days at sea.

Yorktown was well out from Oahu when Captain Buckmaster picked up a microphone and addressed the crew.
The ship, he said, was going to fight one more battle. When

that was over, he had personal orders from Admiral Nimitz to take *Yorktown* and her crew "back to the States." His voice, normally so dispassionate, rose as he concluded: "And not just for any two weeks, either!" Yorktowners burst into cheers. They began counting the time. In two weeks, surely three at most, they would be heading home.

Not long after the captain made his speech, Vane Bennett's radar picked up a flight of aircraft coming out from Hawaii, and lookouts soon had them in their binoculars. Men crowded the catwalks to view a heartwarming sight: more than six dozen airplanes were heading for *Yorktown*'s teakwood deck. Here came the muscle, the power. The planes passed over *Yorktown* in salute, then began peeling off to join the landing circle. Lieutenant Commander Lance Massey led in the fourteen old TBDs of *Saratoga*'s Torpedo 3. Lieutenant Commander Max Leslie led in *Saratoga*'s Bombing 3, with eighteen planes in all. Lieutenant Commander John S. Thach had taken over the fighter squadron, adding himself, a new executive officer, and nine young pilots to the sixteen veteran pilots from Fighting 42 (now Fighting 3). Lieutenant Wally Short, an old Yorktowner, led in nineteen Dauntless dive bombers, now designated Scouting 5.

The planes fell into line and began flying down the carrier's port side. Each made its turn under her stern, the pilot watching the landing signal officer's paddles to determine whether he was high or low or had a wing down. Then, when the LSO gave him the throat cutting signal, he knew he could safely throttle his engine back and land. When Lieutenant Donald Lovelace, Fighting 3's ex-

ecutive officer, swooped in, his Wildcat's tail hook was
quickly freed from the arresting cable, and he taxied forward, out of the way. As he reached a point below Lieutenant Oxy Hurlbert's gunnery platform, catwalk men
pulled on their levers, and a flight-deck barrier rose into
place behind him.

The barrier, a five-foot-high fence of cables, was there
to prevent incoming planes that had missed connecting
with the arresting cables from crashing into planes that
had already landed. The fighter that followed Lovelace's
plane came in high, missing the arresting cable. The pilot
tried to accelerate to pick up flying speed, but he stalled
out and floated over the barrier fence, plunging into the
back of Lovelace's Wildcat. One propeller blade smashed
through Lovelace's headrest, fracturing his skull. The next
blade severed the great arteries in his neck. A pharmacist's
mate rushed to the plane and pinched shut the gash in
Lovelace's neck, but it was too late. "There was nothing
that I or anyone else could do," Dr. Edward Kearney, one
of the medical officers, said afterward.

Chief Wester, who was supposed to know all about the
new fighter planes, had his own problems. These new
Wildcats had folding wings so that more of them could
be stowed aboard aircraft carriers. But when the first Wildcat was freed from the arresting gear, Wester and his men
discovered that they did not know how to fold the wings
back, and he had been given only a single copy of the new
instructional manual to tell him how to operate them. Even
more perplexing, he had no spare parts for the planes, and
the guns had not been boresighted.

The guns were a disappointment. Although the new

Wildcat was equipped with six .50-caliber machine guns, instead of four, the gain in firepower was almost academic. The ammunition supply for the six new guns was only 240 rounds per barrel; each of the four guns on the earlier version had had 450 rounds per barrel.

Yorktown would have to do with what she had, for events were building to a climax. Japanese plans called for the northern force to launch an air attack against Dutch Harbor, in the Aleutians, on June 3. The next day Admiral Nagumo's four big carriers would strike Midway. A day or two later the invasion force would storm ashore.* Only then, Yamamoto probably reasoned, would the American fleet move into action. Nagumo's carriers would hit it hard, and then the great Yamamoto and his battleships would move in for the kill.

Shortly before noon on June 2, *Yorktown* and her escorts, officially called Task Force 17, rendezvoused with *Enterprise* and *Hornet* and their escorts, officially called Task Force 16. Once again, as at the Coral Sea, Admiral Fletcher, in *Yorktown,* took command of the combined fleet. Machinist's Mate George Bateman, up from *Yorktown*'s engine room for a breath of air, was impressed by what he saw. "It sure looked like a lot of power to me," he recalled later, "no matter how big the Jap fleet might be."

Far to the northwest Admiral Nagumo reviewed his final plans in the plotting room aboard his flagship, the carrier

---

* The invasion never took place, but if it had, the defenders on Midway were ready. The atoll was dotted with artillery, and the Marines stationed there were protected by bombproof shelters. The island had almost 3,000 defenders, probably more than enough to stand off the 5,000 Japanese soldiers who were supposed to come ashore. Midway was as carefully prepared for attack as Tarawa would be later in the war, and the attacking force wasn't nearly as impressive as the American force that finally took Tarawa.

Akagi. Nagumo decided to send 100 planes against Midway on June 4 and to hold back an equal number for a second wave, part of which would be composed of torpedo planes. It was the same tactic he had worked to perfection against the British in the Indian Ocean, when he had sunk new targets of opportunity while smashing his main objectives.

Nagumo had many long-ranged scouts working for him, although none of them would be land-based, as at the Coral Sea. The scouts included cruiser and battleship float planes with a range of 600 miles or more. He ordered that seven of these scouts were to keep an eye open for an enemy task force while Midway was being hit; they would cover an arc from due south to northeast. He reasoned that any American force that hoped to strike him while he was attacking Midway would have to be somewhere in that area. If the scouts found such a force, an unlikely event, he thought, the second wave would be dispatched against it. Surely it would be sunk.

Nagumo, all his plans made, turned into his bunk the night of June 2 certain that he had done all he could do. He may even have ceased to worry about the absence of *Shokaku* and *Zuikaku.*

Chapter Ten

★ ★ ★ ★ ★ ★ ★

★ ★ ★ The Battle of Midway opened at 3 A.M. on June 3, more than 1,000 miles north of the atoll itself. Planes from two medium Japanese carriers took off from a point south of the Near and Rat Islands to strike the American base at Dutch Harbor, approximately 250 miles east of the outermost edge of the Aleutian chain.*

Admiral Nimitz, at his Pearl Harbor headquarters, was not fooled by this maneuver. He knew that the main Japanese thrust was heading for Midway, and he wanted to find the enemy ships as quickly as possible. The American search began early on the morning of June 3, when waddling PBY Catalina patrol bombers rumbled down the runways at Midway.

The Catalina was both the joy and despair of American pilots. Parasol-winged and high-tailed, it climbed, flew, and landed at nearly the same speed—about sixty-five knots. Armed only with .30-caliber machine guns in side

---

* The Aleutian campaign is outside the scope of this book. Suffice it to say that both sides blundered in the fog and rain. The Americans were never able to find the enemy ships, and the Japanese failed to entice major U.S. forces from Pearl Harbor to assist the frustrated defenders of the Aleutians. The Japanese did seize Attu and Kiska islands, encountering no resistance whatever, but it was a meaningless conquest.

blisters, the Catalinas were deathtraps when cornered by Japanese fighters. But they had one redeeming feature: they could fly almost all day long without being refueled. Twenty-three of the amphibians were stationed at Midway, assigned to search operations.

The first sighting report was received at 8:43 A.M. from a Catalina pilot, Ensign Jewell Reid, who radioed: "Am investigating suspicious vessels." Twenty-nine minutes later he reported that he could identify "two Japanese cargo vessels," bearing 247 degrees true from Midway. Reid kept shadowing the Japanese vessels until 11 A.M., amplifying his reports until the Midway forces and Admiral Fletcher knew that eleven Japanese ships were west of Midway, steaming toward the island at nineteen knots. Fletcher decided that these ships were unconnected with the carrier striking force he was hoping to find, and he was right—they were part of the Midway occupation force. Nine Army B-17s took off from Midway to attack the convoy, reporting later that they had hit two large warships. They had, in fact, missed again.

Fletcher was certain that the Japanese carriers would approach Midway from the northwest. As soon as the enemy planes began their strike against the island, he hoped to launch an attack against their carriers from his position on their left flank. But at 7:31 P.M. on June 3, with the Japanese attack expected to begin at dawn on June 4, Fletcher had still not located the enemy's carrier force. He ordered *Yorktown, Enterprise,* and *Hornet,* along with their escorts, to change course to the southwest, bringing him closer to Midway, where he could be more certain of intercepting the enemy.

That evening Ship's Cook Renzie Cardin wrote long, loving letters to both the girls to whom he was engaged. Sal Monteleone and a few other diehards started a clandestine crap game. Lieutenant Commanders Jack Delaney and Hubie Strange sat down in *Yorktown's* wardroom for cups of coffee and a discussion of the morrow's weather. As aerologist, Strange had to find prevailing winds to facilitate the launching of planes. If the air was calm, Delaney, as chief engineer, had to turn up enough speed so that *Yorktown* could produce her own wind across the flight deck. As they were discussing these possibilities, Jug Ray, the communications officer, came into the wardroom. He had just left the bridge, and he knew more about Midway battle strategy than most Yorktowners did.

The Alaska strike, he explained to Delaney and Strange, was just a diversionary feint. The ships sighted to the west had been mostly transports; the Japanese carriers had still not been located, not even by the American submarine screen north of Midway. But, said Ray, the carriers would certainly be spotted the next day.

Chief Milt Wester and his mechanics worked through the night on *Yorktown's* fighter planes. By dawn twenty-five would be ready to go, with the two wrecked earlier in the Lovelace landing accident stowed below. Trouble had developed in two torpedo planes during earlier search operations, but they, too, were reported to be repaired and ready to go. At 9 P.M., in a briefing of all pilots, radiomen, and gunners, Lieutenant Dick Cromwell of Fighting 3 gave a speech a bit reminiscent of the talk Jo-Jo Powers had given just before the Coral Sea battle. "The fate of the United States," Cromwell, member of a famous fighting

Navy family, said, "now rests in the hands of two hundred and forty pilots" aboard *Yorktown, Enterprise,* and *Hornet.* He exhorted each man to do his best.

At 1:30 A.M. on June 4 all *Yorktown* airmen ate breakfast. Afterward, Radioman Wendell Anderson, who flew as gunner for Lieutenant Fred Herriman of Torpedo 3, decided to check the condition of his plane, one of the two that had developed trouble the day before. On the flight deck he counted only twelve TBDs; he tried again and still got the same total; it was two fewer than should have been on the line.

He scampered down the ship's ladders to the hangar deck. There were no torpedo planes there, either. Then, looking up, he saw his plane strapped to the overhead where spare or damaged planes were ordinarily hung. "Perhaps," he thought to himself, "they just haven't taken it down yet." To make sure that everything was all right, Anderson climbed up to look the plane over. To his consternation, he found that it had not been touched. He ran to report what he had found to his pilot, Lieutenant Herriman, who in turn reported the news to Lieutenant Commander Lance Massey, the squadron's skipper. Massey soon ran down the trouble—in an almost incredible blunder, no one had been assigned to work on the two torpedo planes. Thus, Torpedo 3 would go into action with twelve planes, instead of fourteen.

At 4:30 A.M. (times used, it should be remembered, are Midway time), the sun rose on *Yorktown's* horizon, just fifteen minutes after eleven Catalinas had taken off from Midway in an attempt to locate the Japanese carriers. At that precise moment, Admiral Chuichi Nagumo's ships were making twenty knots on the final run to their launching point. *Akagi*, Nagumo's flagship, was only a little more than 200 miles west of *Yorktown*.

Rising with the sun were ten of Lieutenant Wally Short's dive bombers, ordered to search 100 miles in a northern semicircle, west to east. The rest of the dive bombers, on the three carriers, were standing by to go after whatever Short's SBDs might find. All Short's flight encountered, however, were enemy float planes. Ensign Ben Preston tangled with one, without discernible result.

At the same time that Short's search party was taking off, 36 Zeros were rising from the decks of Nagumo's four carriers. They circled overhead while 36 torpedo planes (carrying bombs for this strike) and 36 dive bombers rose to join them. Then, at 5 A.M., all 108 planes steadied on a course for Midway. Lieutenant Joichi Tomonaga, air group commander from *Hiryu*, led them in.

Sixteen B-17s were taking off at the same time from Midway on a search-strike effort. Also in the air were two Japanese float planes from the heavy cruiser *Tone*, two from the heavy cruiser *Chikuma*, one from the battleship *Haruna*, and a torpedo plane from each of the two carriers, *Kaga* and *Akagi*.

At 5:20 A.M., Nagumo signaled all his ships that he might send a second wave against Midway soon after the first wave attacked. As signalmen blinked his message, 152 aircraft from both sides were already in the air, itching for a fight.

At 5:30 A.M., Nagumo was spotted by a Catalina. The pilot radioed Midway that he had one Japanese carrier in sight, bearing 320 degrees from the island, distance 150 miles. *Enterprise* intercepted the message and relayed it to *Yorktown*. Although Nagumo's fleet had now kicked its speed up to twenty-six knots, both Fletcher and Spruance knew roughly what his location was. Minutes later a second PBY radioed a message, this one not even coded. "Many planes headed Midway," the pilot reported, in clear English. "Repeat, Midway, bearing three hundred and twenty degrees true, distance one hundred and fifty miles."

Every plane on Midway was ordered into the air, some to attack the enemy carriers, some to intercept the incoming planes, some simply to be removed out of the way.

Fighters from all four Japanese carriers were sent aloft to track down the Catalina that was giving away their location. But the amphibian evaded them all by ducking in and out of the clouds. It was not long before it was joined by other Catalinas. From that moment on, Nagumo's carriers were kept under almost constant surveillance.

At 6 A.M. the only plane left on Midway was an ancient Grumman single-float biplane. Six new Grumman Avenger torpedo bombers, accompanied by four Army B-26 bombers, were streaking northwest toward the enemy carriers. Midway radio also ordered the sixteen B-17s already in the air to turn north and strike the enemy force. At 6:07 Fletcher ordered Spruance to steam southwest with *Enterprise* and *Hornet* and attack the enemy carriers as soon as he saw fit. "I will follow," Fletcher said, "as soon as our search planes are recovered." Once committed, Fletcher planned to dispatch one strike group, holding back a second to await developments.

By 6:30 A.M. *Yorktown*'s crew was at battle stations, and

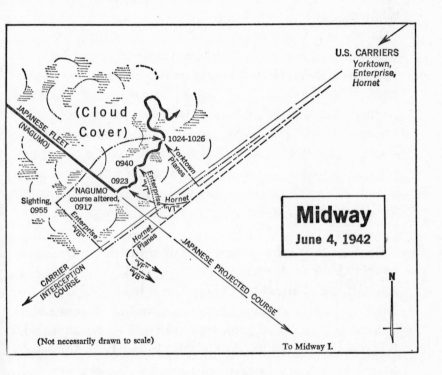

U.S. CARRIERS
Yorktown,
Enterprise,
Hornet

JAPANESE FLEET
(NAGUMO)

(Cloud Cover)

1024-1026

Yorktown Planes

0940

0923

Enterprise "VT"

Hornet "VT"

NAGUMO course altered, 0917

Sighting, 0955

Enterprise "VB"

Hornet Planes

"VF"
"VB"

CARRIER INTERCEPTION COURSE

JAPANESE PROJECTED COURSE

Midway
June 4, 1942

N

(Not necessarily drawn to scale)

To Midway I.

bombs had begun dropping on Midway. Marine Corps fighters—obsolescent Brewster Buffalos—tried to fend off the Japanese attackers, but they were no match for the Zeros. Fifteen of the twenty-five Buffalos were shot down, and of the ten that survived, seven were so battered that they would never fly again.

Lieutenant Commander Yahachi Tanabe, skipper of the Japanese submarine *I-168*, had a ringside seat for the Midway show. His submarine was prowling ten miles south of Sand Island. "The island," he wrote after the war, "turned into a mass of flames, with exploding fuel tanks and military buildings. We saw it become covered with flames and a thick, black smoke. I let my navigator, communications officer, gunnery officer, and a few others take a turn looking through the periscope." A cheer burst from the crew when Tanabe announced that a large fuel tank had exploded.

At 6:55 A.M. the Japanese strike, nearly intact, was heading back to its carriers. Damage to Midway had been considerable. Barracks buildings, mess halls, and even the hospital had been hit. The explosion that Commander Tanabe had seen had been from oil tanks on Sand Island. But the island's ability to fight back had been little impaired. Only a few bombs had landed on the runway, and the damage they had caused was easily and quickly repaired. Casualties on the ground were remarkably light.

Lieutenant Joichi Tomonaga, leading the Japanese strike back to the carriers, radioed Admiral Nagumo that another strike would be needed to soften up the island for a ship-to-shore assault. Admiral Nagumo had already spotted his second strike on his decks; it was composed of fighters, dive bombers, and torpedo planes. He knew, of course, that if he sent them away, he would have hardly anything left to send against enemy surface ships, should his scouts spot any. Nagumo began to miss *Zuikaku* and *Shokaku* and the 120 to 140 additional planes they would have provided him.

As the admiral paced the flag bridge of *Akagi,* pondering his next move, over the horizon there came American planes—the torpedo-carrying Avengers and B-26s from Midway, ten in all. They dropped their torpedoes, and *Akagi* nimbly dodged three of them. Other carriers dodged the rest. Zeros then shot down five of the Grummans and two of the B-26s; only three planes of the original ten made it back to Midway. They had not scored one hit on the enemy.

At 7:15 A.M., Nagumo reached his decision. He would hit Midway again and eliminate the possibility of more land-based attacks on his fleet. To all carriers went a message from the flag bridge: "Planes in the second wave, stand by to carry out attack." Then he added: "Reload with bombs."

This second order threw the decks of *Kaga* and *Akagi* into crazy confusion. Each of those two carriers had eighteen planes loaded with torpedoes and spotted ready for takeoff in case an enemy surface fleet was sighted. Now all thirty-six planes had to be taken below, their torpedoes removed, and bombs slung in their places. Then the planes had to be brought back up to the flight decks.

Most writers insist that this was a colossal blunder, perhaps even the mistake that lost the war. Yet in context it was a reasonable decision. Midway obviously had to be struck again, for after all, planes from Midway had just attacked Nagumo's own ship. Besides, at the moment the decision was made, Japanese scouts had found no sign of an enemy surface fleet in the area where Nagumo thought such a fleet was most likely to be.

So, Nagumo reasoned, sending another wave against Midway would be no gamble. His first wave would soon be back, to replace those planes he would now send away. He could load bombs and torpedoes on the planes of the first wave as soon as they came home and be ready for surface ships whenever his scouts found them. Viewed objectively, it was a logical decision. At 7:15 A.M., Japanese flight officers on *Kaga* and *Akagi* broke the spot—that is, pulled apart the arrangement of planes on their decks.

The versatile Nakajima-97 bombers were swiftly taken below, their torpedoes were rapidly removed and trundled away to be stacked along the sides of the hangar decks. There was no time to observe even the most fundamental safety precautions, no time at all to stow the torpedoes below in armored magazines. They were going right back on other planes within the hour. The important task, Japanese officers knew, was to get the Nakajimas, now armed with bombs, back up to the flight deck and into the air.

At 7:28 A.M., while this was going on, Nagumo received the worst possible news. A scout plane from the cruiser *Tone* radioed: "Have sighted an estimated ten ships, bearing zero ten degrees true, distance two hundred and forty miles from Midway." He added that they were heading southwest, at more than twenty knots. Aboard *Astoria*, one of the ships spotted by the scout, a quartermaster logged at about this time that the sea was calm and the sky clear, except for a small sprinkling of clouds on the horizon. Those clouds concealed the Japanese snooper.

Nagumo began pacing the flag bridge again. At 7:45 he issued more orders. The first went to the patrolling scout: "Ascertain the types of ships." So far he did not know whether the enemy fleet contained aircraft carriers. In his second order he instructed his own fleet to "prepare to carry out attack on enemy fleet units." He added: "Leave torpedoes on those planes which have not already changed to bombs."

Just as Nagumo was trying to think out his plans, he was interrupted again by American bombers. This time it was sixteen Marine Corps Dauntless dive bombers from Midway. Their commander, knowing that his young pilots had no experience in steep diving, had brought the planes in on a glide. Zeros knocked eight of them down almost instantly. The rest barely made it back to Midway. Not a single hit was scored on the Japanese fleet. No sooner had the dive bombers been beaten off than the sixteen Army B-17s appeared over Nagumo's fleet and began dropping bombs from 20,000 feet. Pilots of the B-17s, watching the bombs splash almost 4 miles below, were certain that they had scored important hits; they wheeled around and headed triumphantly home. Before the battle was even over, one Army pilot managed to get to Honolulu and claim over Honolulu radio that the B-17s had scored heavily. But it was the same old story. They had not even come close to doing so.

Other planes came roaring out of Midway. This time it was a flight of eleven Vought SB2U Vindicators, manned by Marines. These old planes, partly covered by canvas, had long been rejected by Navy carrier pilots. The Vindicators, making their runs, were severely punished by Zeros, to the point where the pilots could hardly take aim. All their bombs missed, and the Vindicators limped back toward Midway. The surprise was that nine of them got back home again.

At this point Nagumo had been attacked by fifty-two American planes and one submarine and had not been scratched.* Nagumo, it seemed, could congratulate himself on the way the battle was going. At 8:20 A.M. he heard again from his scout, who reported to him that the enemy force was accompanied "by what appears to be an aircraft carrier." (It was an aircraft carrier—*Yorktown*.) Still, Nagumo could measure distance accurately enough, and even if the scout were right, the carrier was still at extreme fighting range. He had time to consider his next moves.

The time was approaching 8:30, and the returning Japanese attack wave was beginning to arrive overhead. Fresh thoughts began to occur to Nagumo. If he recovered these planes and rearmed them, he would be as strong as he had been when he had launched the first wave. He would again have two strike waves at the ready. At 8:30 he issued further orders. Clear the flight decks, he commanded, and bring in the first wave. Had it not been for the iron discipline taught early to all Japanese sailors, the men aboard the four carriers might have cursed Nagumo aloud. As it was, they went back to work, breaking the spot all over again. More haste and carelessness were the

* The submarine was *Nautilus*. She got off one torpedo at a battleship and then, amid the crash of depth bombs, ran for her life. But she was to return to fight another time.

result on *Kaga* and *Akagi*. Bombs, as well as torpedoes, were now stacked along the sides of the hangar deck, instead of being stowed safely below.

Nagumo could not know it, but his carriers were shortly to pay dearly for his hesitation and the crews' haste.

Chapter Eleven

★ ★ ★ ★ ★ ★ ★

★ ★ ★ First, however, the Americans were to offer their torpedo planes in bloody sacrifice.

Three torpedo squadrons took after the Japanese fleet —Torpedo 6 from *Enterprise* (fourteen planes), Torpedo 8 from *Hornet* (fifteen planes), and Torpedo 3 from *Yorktown* (twelve planes).

The skipper of Torpedo 8, Lieutenant Commander John C. Waldron, was a brave and stubborn man. He had no sooner taken off from *Hornet* than he decided to ignore his orders and set his own course for the point where he was convinced he would find the Japanese fleet. He veered right soon after takeoff, whereas *Hornet*'s dive bombers and fighters pushed straight ahead. Within minutes they had lost Waldron and his torpedo planes in the clouds.

Torpedo 8 found the Japanese sooner than anyone else, but Waldron and his men were all alone, without a single fighter plane as cover. At 9:25 A.M. the fifteen TBDs began their attack. As Oscar Pederson had feared, the Japanese had learned to protect their carriers properly, so Waldron's squadron was forced to push through fire from the widespread escorts, from the carriers themselves, and from a defending swarm of Zeros.

In five minutes the Japanese had shot down all fifteen planes. Of the thirty men from Torpedo 8, courageous men who had taken an oath to defend the United States "against all enemies, whomsoever," twenty-nine died. The only survivor was Ensign George Gay, pilot of the last plane in line. Gay pressed forward, trying for a hit, until Zeros killed his radioman and shot down his plane. Wounded, he crawled from the TBD and clung for hours to a seat cushion that had floated free from the plane. It was not until darkness descended that Gay dared inflate his life raft. No Torpedo 8 plane scored a hit.

Hornet's dive bombers and fighters, forty-five in all, missed the battle entirely. When they reached the projected path of the Japanese fleet, they swung southeast, thinking that the enemy fleet had already passed the interception point. Thirteen of the dive bombers, short on fuel, had to make forced landings on Midway. Two of them ran out of gas and had to ditch. All of *Hornet's* fighters ran out of gas and ditched in the ocean. *Hornet* was out of it, all her strike planes either shot down or forced down.

Left in the air, however, were the squadrons from *Yorktown* and *Enterprise*. This was the first team, and it was going to score.

After Torpedo 8's attack, events began to pile up in rapid and confusing order, and it may well be advantageous to take a moment to set the scene.

Yorktown had laid back to collect her ten search scouts. *Enterprise* and *Hornet*, at Fletcher's behest, had dashed ahead. Soon the two task forces lost visual contact with each other. From that moment on, they functioned almost as independent units. By the time Japanese scouts sighted *Yorktown,* the other two carriers had slipped over the horizon. The Japanese did not find those two carriers until it was much too late to do anything about it. *Yorktown,* however, could not shake the enemy snoopers, particularly the float plane from the cruiser *Tone.* It's pilot radioed the word when *Yorktown* launched its strike, and he then began to beam a homing radio signal to be used, when the time came, to guide a Japanese strike directly to *Yorktown.* Thus, *Yorktown,* from the moment the battle began, was a marked ship.

A major problem aboard all three American carriers was navigational—how best to intercept the Japanese fleet. Of all the three ships, *Yorktown* solved it best, so that, alone, her strike went in with all planes present and accounted for. It was a splendid piece of work, and the credit goes to Hubie Strange, the weatherman, and Oscar Pederson, the air group commander, two men never before mentioned in any published account of the Midway battle.

Strange was unable to prepare a reliable weather map because the United States had no weather station west of Midway. He knew, however, that the winds were blowing between *Yorktown* and the Japanese fleet and that these winds could be of different speeds and moving from different directions, at different altitudes. Strange advised *Yorktown's* pilots to watch the wind streaks on the surface of the ocean and to correct for drift by observing any wind changes. This observation would be made by the torpedo squadron under Lieutenant Commander Lance Massey, for it flew much lower than the dive bombers and fighters. The higher F4Fs and SBDs, simply by keeping tabs on the TBDs thousands of feet below them, could easily stay on proper course, too.

Pederson, just prior to the takeoff of *Yorktown*'s strike, determined that the enemy fleet would be 156 miles southwest of *Yorktown*, heading southeast into the wind and toward Midway. The Japanese would continue on that course, he believed, because they had to head into the wind to launch and to retrieve their planes. Pederson proposed that *Yorktown*'s pilots assume that the Japanese fleet was steaming at *very* high speed. An interception point was then plotted out, based on the best speed the Japanese could possibly make. If, when *Yorktown*'s planes arrived over the interception point, the Japanese fleet was nowhere in sight, there could be only one answer: the Japanese fleet was sure to be directly to the northwest, steaming down the preplotted line of advance. All *Yorktown*'s planes would have to do, according to Pederson's theory, would be to turn up that line of advance and watch for the enemy's smoke.

Admiral Fletcher, at 8:30 A.M., had come to a decision of his own. Remembering Admiral Nimitz's orders to "inflict maximum damage . . . by the principle of calculated risk," Fletcher ordered Buckmaster to throw more than half his aircraft into the battle, even though he was not certain that other Japanese carriers were not lurking over the horizon still unreported.

Buckmaster ordered the seventeen planes of Bombing 3, under Lieutenant Commander Max Leslie, the twelve planes of Torpedo 3, under Lance Massey, and six Wildcats, under Lieutenant Commander John S. Thach, to make the attack. Nineteen Wildcats were held back to rotate over *Yorktown* as air cover. Wally Short's Scouting 5 remained aboard to await developments. Max Leslie's dive bombers took off first and circled overhead as Lance Massey's torpedo planes were launched. Seaman John Ginn, from his station at a forward 1.1-inch gun mount, waved wildly to a hometown friend, Radioman Raymond Darcy, as Darcy's plane rolled by. Neither Darcy nor his plane would return. *Yorktown's* strike was in the air by 9:06 A.M. No sooner had they gone than *Yorktown* respotted the flight deck with six fighters and Wally Short's seventeen dive bombers. Fletcher wanted to be ready to strike a second blow.

Strikes from *Enterprise* and *Hornet* were already in the air. They had got off in some disarray because Fighting 6, the Wildcat squadron from *Enterprise*, had mistakenly attached itself to Torpedo 8 from *Hornet*. Fighting 6's commander, Lieutenant James Gray, had been instructed prior to takeoff to remain at high altitude to protect the attacking dive bombers from both *Hornet* and *Enterprise*. But *Hornet's* planes had turned the wrong way, and *Enterprise's* dive bombers were late getting into battle. Gray, as a result, found himself over the Japanese fleet with no dive bombers to protect; down below, he could see the torpedo planes making their suicidal runs. He was at the point of no return, owing to the mix-up, and did not have enough spare gas left to attempt to help them. Gray finally radioed Lieutenant Commander Clarence McClusky, skipper of *Enterprise's* dive bombers, that he was short of fuel and had to head home. He could do nothing else.

So it was that the fourteen planes of Torpedo 6, from *Enterprise*, attacked without fighter cover. *Enterprise*'s planes began their runs at 9:51 A.M. Nine minutes later, ten of them, including Skipper Eugene Lindsay's, were down. The remaining four were badly battered and only barely made a getaway. Again, not a single torpedo had scored a hit on the enemy.

Yorktown's planes, despite their late start, began arriving over the Japanese fleet by 10 A.M., thanks to the advice the pilots had received from Strange and Pederson.

Four of *Yorktown*'s dive bombers had no bombs, for not long before the battle began, the *Yorktown* dive bombers had been equipped with a new device to arm and release their bombs. Lieutenant Commander Max Leslie, Bombing 3's skipper, reached down to pull the arming lever as he was en route to the target. As soon as he pulled it, he felt his Dauntless leap upward. On Leslie's wing, Lieutenant Paul "Swede" Holmberg watched in dismay as Leslie's 1,000-pound bomb fell away into an empty ocean. The same thing happened to Ensigns Roy Isaman, Charles Lane, and Bud Merrill. After the battle the trouble was diagnosed: someone had erroneously crossed the wires when he had installed the electric bomb armers so that a pull on the arming lever actually released the bomb instead of arming it.

Of the *Yorktown* squadrons, Torpedo 3 was the first to sight the enemy. Lance Massey, because he was close to the water, had a clear view, and he spotted the smoke that had been laid down by Japanese destroyers during the earlier attack by Torpedo 8. Massey changed his squadron's course about thirty degrees to the right to make an attack from the north of the Japanese squadron, nose to nose with the enemy carriers. About 5,000 feet above *Yorktown's* torpedo planes were Commander Thach's six Grumman Wildcats, hoping to cover their shipmates below.

They never had a chance. A shellburst, probably from a Japanese cruiser, pinpointed their location and led Zeros right to the little group. Thach and the five other pilots were jumped by about fifteen Zeros. A wild scramble followed—the only fighter plane action that occurred over the Japanese fleet—and one Wildcat, piloted by Ed Bassett, was shot down.

Thach's dogfight and the Torpedo 3 attack that began minutes later had an exceedingly important relationship to the final outcome of the battle, even though both these incidents have been almost totally neglected by naval historians. All accounts of the battle, including Admiral Morison's, state flatly that Torpedo 8 and Torpedo 6, in sacrificing themselves, drew defending Zeros swarming down to sea level, thus permitting the American dive bombers to make their target runs almost unmolested. This is not so; Torpedo 8 and Torpedo 6 did not perform this useful service. In fact, most of the Zeros had plenty of time to regain altitude after the two torpedo attacks. What drew many of them away from the dive bombers was the six Wildcats led by Commander Thach. Most of the remaining Zeros were drawn away by the attack launched by Torpedo 3, also from *Yorktown*.

It is important to place the Japanese carriers in their proper positions. At first sighting by *Yorktown* planes, they were in a loose box formation, heading north. *Hiryu* and *Kaga* were deployed to the east, *Soryu* and *Akagi* to the west. To put it another way, *Hiryu* and *Soryu,* the two medium carriers, were out ahead, followed by *Kaga* and *Akagi.* Both of the latter carriers, like *Lexington* and *Saratoga,* were immense ships that had been converted from battle cruisers.

Hiryu was far ahead of the three other carriers, and the higher-flying American planes could not see her because she had moved under some clouds. Lance Massey, leading *Yorktown's* Torpedo 3, spotted her, however, and made his attack against her. He formed Torpedo 3 into two divisions of six planes each. Leslie wanted to catch *Hiryu* between a cross fire from these two divisions.

Harry Corl was one of two Torpedo 3 pilots who survived the attack. Japanese fighter planes began to jump them, he reported, even before Torpedo 3 reached the outer screen of Japanese ships. He estimated that Torpedo 3 was attacked by about twenty-four Zeros. With another dozen or so dogfighting Thach, this means that thirty-six Japanese fighters, almost all the Japanese fleet's air cover, were working over the sixteen planes from *Yorktown.* And that is why the *Yorktown* (and, later, *Enterprise*) dive bombers were able to start their runs without interference.

Small consolation it was to the men of Torpedo 3. The other pilot who survived was Wilhelm Esders, whose position was just to the rear and left of Commander Massey. The Zeros began attacking the formation when it was still 14 miles northeast of the main Japanese fleet and when the torpedo planes were still flying at 2,600 feet.

"I saw the Zero that shot the skipper down as he made his approach," Esders said. "I was slightly step-down, and two Zeros had both the skipper's and my plane in line when they began firing, approaching from the skipper's starboard bow. Realizing they could get us both in one pass, I immediately stepped up in formation, and the bullets, including tracers, passed just under my place. Both Zeros came from the same direction. The skipper's plane immediately burst into flames." Esders watched as Massey tried to climb out of his plane, apparently hoping to parachute. But he was only 150 feet off the water. Esders, when his skipper went down, took over lead spot in the formation. He heard what "sounded like hundreds of bullets" passing through his plane, some of them exploding inside it. He was thankful for the homemade armor—boiler plate from the shops at Kaneohe, Oahu—that had recently been installed. Esders could hear the bullets bouncing off it.

Esders continued to press the attack, just as the hopeless men of Torpedo 8 and Torpedo 6 had done before him. Friendly planes disappeared—first Massey; then Richard Suesens, Wesley Osmus, and David Roche. Harry Corl, the other survivor, tried to follow Esders, but his elevator controls were so damaged by gunfire that he could not keep his plane's nose down. He had to jettison his torpedo and break away.

The second division, led by Lieutenant Pat Hart, was wiped out. Down with his went the planes of John Haas, Oswald Powers, Leonard Smith, Curt Howard, and Carl Osberg. "I recall seeing four planes of the second division off to my right," Esders said, "and I saw two of them crash. I don't believe any of those planes ever arrived in position to drop their torpedoes, and I don't think any of the first-division planes got to position to drop their torpedoes except my own plane." Esders, a chief petty officer (this was in the day when many Navy pilots were still enlisted men), let go his torpedo about 500 yards from *Hiryu,* but somehow the carrier evaded it. Esders then swung 180 degrees to the right and headed away from *Hiryu.* To his left he could see three surviving torpedo planes. One of them probably was Harry Corl's. Two of the three planes were shot down a few minutes later.

Esders and Corl ran north, trying to lure the Zeros still farther away from the main concentration of ships. All the time both rear gunners—Lloyd Childers for Corl and Mike Brazier for Esders—kept shooting, even though they were both wounded. Childers, when his .30-caliber machine gun jammed, opened up on the pursuing Zeros with a .45-caliber pistol.

It was now past 10:20 A.M., and the Japanese fleet was still untouched, even though 52 planes had attacked from Midway, a submarine had fired a torpedo, and 41 torpedo planes had flown strikes against it from American carriers.

Altogether, Fletcher's carriers sent 152 planes against the Japanese task force. Of these, 45 from *Hornet* went the wrong way. That left 107. Waldron and all but one of his Torpedo 8 comrades were dead, and their planes gone. That left 92. Of these, 10 torpedo planes from *Enterprise* were gone, and 4 others were limping home. That left 78. Thach's Wildcats were trying to fight off a swarm of Zeros; that made it 72. *Enterprise's* 10 fighters, low on fuel, were heading home. So 62 were left. And now 10 of Massey's planes were in the ocean, with two survivors trying to get home.

That left only 50 planes, less than a third of the American strike, to start the job, for so far no one had inflicted any damage at all.

Shortly after 10 A.M. the 33 dive bombers from *Enterprise* got a break. Lieutenant Commander Clarence McClusky, their skipper, spotted an enemy destroyer through the clouds; the destroyer, alone, was hightailing it for somewhere. The destroyer was *Arashi*, speeding northeast to rejoin Nagumo's formation after trying to run down an American submarine contact. McClusky reasoned that the destroyer was probably heading for the Japanese fleet, so he pointed himself in the same direction. He arrived over the task force at 10:24 A.M.

Of the many accounts that have been written about the Battle of Midway, all but one credit *Enterprise*'s dive bombers with being the first to hit a Japanese carrier on that historic June 4, 1942. Japanese postwar accounts agree. No doubt about it, everyone has said, *Enterprise* was first. The lone dissenter, until now, has been Professor Thaddeus V. Tuleja, of St. Peter's College, Jersey City, New Jersey. The professor is correct. *Enterprise*—the glamorous Big E—did *not* score the first hit. *Yorktown*—neglected, ragged Old Yorky—was the first to do so.

Chapter Twelve

★ ★ ★ ★ ★ ★ ★

★ ★ ★ It is typical that *Yorktown* should have scored first against the Japanese at Midway; she had been first all along. But it is also typical that the man who led the attack should have been flying a dive bomber with no bomb. *Yorktown* had never done things the easy way.

Max Leslie, skipper of *Yorktown's* Bombing 3, had turned north, too, when Lance Massey and the forlorn torpedo bombers veered to make their run. Leslie radioed Massey, trying to find out whether the torpedo planes had seen anything, but he received no reply. An answer became unnecessary when Leslie's gunner, W. E. Gallagher, called to him and pointed out ships, dead ahead, about thirty miles away. *Yorktown's* planes, every one of them, had found the enemy, and they were, more or less, together when they did it.

Leslie began easing down to 14,500 feet, wondering what to do next. Here he was in the lead, but he had no bomb. Should he give over his lead position to one of the thirteen planes that still had bombs? He thought about it a moment and rejected the idea. Bombing 3, he concluded, should have its dive course set by the most experienced pilot in the squadron—himself.

At 10:23 A.M. *Yorktown's* dive bombers were over the easternmost portion of the Japanese fleet. No Zeros were there to oppose them, for they were busy with Thach's Wildcats above the center of the Japanese force and Massey's torpedo planes well to the northeast. Below Leslie's squadron was an immense aircraft carrier. Despite what others have written, this carrier was *Kaga*, one of the former battle cruisers.* Two other carriers—*Akagi* (Nagumo's flagship) and *Soryu*—were well to the west. *Hiryu*, the carrier attacked by *Yorktown's* torpedo planes, was under clouds and out of sight to the north.

Leslie glanced out of his cockpit and caught the eye of his wingman, Swede Holmberg. Then he patted his helmet in the familiar aviator's signal meaning "I've got it." He nosed his Dauntless over and began his dive, *Yorktown's* sixteen other bombers falling into line behind him. Leslie aimed straight at the big red rising sun that decorated *Kaga's* flight deck. During his dive he opened up with his forward-firing .50-caliber machine guns, pumping 400 to 500 rounds into the area around the carrier's starboard bridge. Seconds after his guns jammed at 4,000 feet, he began pulling out.

Right behind him was Swede Holmberg, who later recalled watching in fascination "lights blinking all around the edge of that dark red flight deck." It was antiaircraft fire, of course, and Holmberg soon heard shrapnel rat-

---

* Morison says that *Enterprise's* McClusky was the first to attack and that he went after *Kaga*. *Yorktown*, Morison writes, came in later and went after *Soryu*. In fact, the situation was just the reverse. Professor Tuleja, again, has reconstructed the actual events correctly.

tling through his plane "like rocks on a tin roof." When
Leslie pulled out, Holmberg got a clear look at his target.
"It was the biggest thing I ever saw," Holmberg said.
Taking no chance on equipment failure, he pulled both
his electrical and manual bomb releases. A 1,000-pound
delayed-action bomb fell gently away from the plane's
belly.

The bomb, first American blow at Midway to land, hit
squarely in the middle of the rising sun insignia on *Kaga's*
flight deck. Right behind Holmberg was Ensign Paul
Schlegel. He saw *Kaga's* deck "burst apart." Then he re-
leased his bomb; so did Bob Campbell, Oley Hansen,
Bob Benson, and Gordon Sherwood. Eighth in line was
Ensign Roy Isaman, piloting another bombless bomber.
He sprayed with his machine guns, just as Leslie had done.
Next came Phil Cobb, Sid Bottomley, and Charles Lane.
Lane, bombless too, sprayed more machine gun fire over
Kaga.

At this point eight bombs had been dropped. Leslie,
pulling away, looked back and saw the explosion from
Holmberg's bomb. It had crashed through the flight deck
and detonated in the hangar deck. The explosion was followed by two more, each successively larger. The bombs
and torpedoes which had been pushed aside by *Kaga's*
ordnancemen after they had twice broken the spot were
going off. Airplanes were blowing up on both the flight and
the hangar decks.

The last six SBDs in the line of attack were piloted by
John Butler, David "Dave" Shumway, Bob Elder, Randy
Cooner, Obie Wiseman, and Bud Merrill. Butler saw that
the carrier was in very bad shape, so he veered off toward

a battleship. Wiseman followed him after the same target. Elder and Cooner went after what they thought was a light cruiser. Shumway, the squadron's executive officer, maintained his course for *Kaga*, hoping to deliver the crusher. Merrill, last in the line, flew almost in Shumway's prop wash, pushing the attack, even though he, too, had no bomb. Because his was the last plane in, *Kaga*'s gunners concentrated all their fire on him; somehow, he survived.

Yorktown's dive bombers, their work done, headed for home as fast as they could go, hugging the ocean's surface so that enemy fighters could not get under them. Ensign Roy Isaman's plane was attacked by a twin-float seaplane, but his gunner, Sidney Weaver, drove it off. Behind Bombing 3, *Kaga* was an "inferno of flame," as Lieutenant Shumway later noted in his action report.

Bombing 3 had done incredibly well. Captured Japanese documents later showed that the squadron's planes scored four hits out of nine bombs dropped at *Kaga* and that three of the misses were very close indeed, exploding just off the carrier's port side, forward. The other two bombs came almost as close on *Kaga*'s starboard side. *Kaga*, when attacked, was twisting at thirty knots; scoring four hits out of nine attempts on that kind of target and laying five more close aboard were a performance even the Japanese could admire. They did, later, in reports and postwar interviews.

Yorktown pilots struck Nagumo the first blow. *Enterprise* pilots struck the second and third blows. Aboard *Akagi*, there was hardly time to note in the ship's log that "*Kaga* is under attack" before bombs began dropping on the flagship.

Commander McClusky, leading the thirty-three bombers

from *Enterprise,* split his force in two, sending one division after *Akagi* and the other after *Soryu* (he did not know the names of the carriers at the time of the attack, of course). By 10:26 *Akagi* had been hit twice and *Soryu* three times. By 10:30 all the Japanese carriers, except *Hiryu,* were burning furiously. *Hiryu,* still protected by the clouds she had run under, was not seen by any of the fifty American dive bombers until their attacks were over and they were heading home, at low altitude. Some of the American planes made her out, on the northern horizon, but it was too late to do anything about it; none of them had any bombs left.

All of *Yorktown's* dive bombers got away. *Enterprise's* planes were not so lucky. Only eighteen out of the original force of thirty-three made it back to their ship. "It may have been because they were over a thicker group of ships than we were and had more opposition," *Yorktown* pilot Sid Bottomley theorized. Another factor was a shortage of fuel; some of *Enterprise's* planes, not as well directed to the Japanese ships as *Yorktown's* were by Strange and Pederson, simply ran out of gas. Six pilots and five rear gunners were later plucked from the sea.

Yorktown's Commander Thach, fighting off Zeros, managed to get an occasional look at what was happening below. When he finally started back for *Yorktown,* he had a clear picture of three Japanese carriers burning wildly and shuddering from explosions that sent flames and smoke billowing into the sky.

The Japanese situation was as desperate as it looked. *Kaga's* planes were blowing up like a string of firecrackers. *Akagi* was in such bad shape that Nagumo was forced to abandon her. He took his flag and the sacrosanct portrait of the emperor to the light cruiser *Nagara*. The captain of *Soryu* abandoned ship at 10:45 A.M. But *Hiryu*, still untouched, had a fighting commander on board—Rear Admiral Tamon Yamaguchi—and he had no intention of giving up. Yamaguchi, involved in a spy scandal while serving in Washington in the 1930's, had been touted as the logical successor to the great Yamamoto as commander in chief of the Japanese fleet. Earlier in the day, when the first sighting of American ships had been reported, Yamaguchi had urged Nagumo to strike immediately; his message had been worded in language that bordered on the insulting. Rebuffed then, he now seized his opportunity. At 11:09 A.M. he notified all the ships in the fleet that *Hiryu*'s planes were going to "destroy the American aircraft carrier." A minute later he signaled that his first air strike was off and that it would be followed by a second within the hour.

Still on the job were the snoopers—Catalinas over the Japanese fleet, Japanese float planes over *Yorktown*. The original Japanese scout, from the cruiser *Tone*, remained on station until its courageous pilot, who has never been identified, reported that he had only fifty-one gallons of fuel left. He then turned for home, and his place was taken by a float plane from the cruiser *Chikuma* and a special high-speed scout from *Hiryu*. Two of these scouts never saw *Enterprise* or *Hornet*; the third did, but his radio messages apparently failed to get through. The result was that all the available surviving Japanese planes concentrated on *Yorktown*.

At 11:15 A.M. *Yorktown*'s returning dive bombers began

arriving over their ship. Two *Enterprise* planes, badly damaged, were taken aboard, and Thach's five surviving Wildcats landed.* One of them, piloted by T. F. Cheek, crash-landed. "The plane did a cartwheel right below my battle station on the stack and then slammed into the barrier," Seaman George Weise later recalled. The accident delayed landing operations; the seventeen dive bombers had to circle overhead while the flight deck was being cleared. Circling not far away, too, was the float plane from the cruiser *Chikuma*. The pilot radioed a weather report. "Clear," it said, "with half of the sky covered by clouds. Their [the clouds'] bases are twenty-four hundred to three thousand feet above the surface. Wind is from the east, fifteen meters per second, and visibility is thirty miles." Conditions for a dive bomber attack could hardly have been better.

Yorktown's flight deck was cleared at 11:50 A.M., and ten of Lieutenant Wally Short's dive bombers were ordered out on a search for the fourth carrier that the attacking planes had belatedly sighted. Short's planes were to search a distance of 250 miles in an arc from due west to a little past north. With the scouts away, Commander Pederson set about recovering Bombing 3. He never got the chance, for at 11:59 A.M. *Yorktown's* radar picked up enemy planes coming in from just south of west, distance 46 miles.

Vane Bennett, the radar boss, turned to his assistant, Speedy Attaway, and said, "Well, here we go again!"

---

* Thach immediately reported to Admiral Fletcher. *Yorktown* jubilantly signaled other ships that her planes had sunk a carrier. The claim was premature, but, ultimately, accurate enough.

The Japanese planes had got within forty-six miles of *Yorktown* without being spotted by flying low; that put them under the straight-line beam of Bennett's crude radar. At the Coral Sea they had been flying high and had been picked up at sixty-eight miles. This, not explained in earlier accounts of the Midway battle, shows why they got closer, undetected, in the second battle. At about the time that they were picked up, they began climbing to the altitude from which they would begin their dives.

Aboard *Yorktown* certain precautions suggested by Machinist Oscar Myers after the Battle of the Coral Sea were put into effect. Fueling of Wildcats on the flight decks was stopped. All gasoline lines were drained, then charged with nonflammable carbon dioxide at 20 pounds' pressure. Myers saw to it that an auxiliary gasoline tank, loaded with 800 gallons of high octane fuel, was pushed over *Yorktown's* stern. *Lexington*, Myers remembered, had been swept by fires sparked by ruptured gas lines and gas tanks. The same thing would not happen to *Yorktown* if he could help it.

Below, in *Yorktown's* main engine room, Jack Delaney watched in near disbelief as the pitometer log indicator crept up toward thirty knots. When the temporary repairs had been made at Pearl Harbor, no one, not in his wildest dreams, had thought that *Yorktown* would be able to make anything above twenty-seven knots without her superheater boilers.

The heavy cruisers *Astoria* and *Portland* and the destroyers *Hammann*, *Anderson*, *Russell*, *Morris*, and *Hughes* took Cruising Disposition Victor, a defensive ring around *Yorktown*. This screened the carrier from subma-rine attack and added their guns to the antiaircraft defense. At high noon Captain Buckmaster ordered a quartermaster to break out *Yorktown*'s battle flag, the largest national ensign aboard the ship. Seaman Warren Woodard hauled it up to the gaff. Electrician's Mate Leroy Gill, at his battle station on the bridge, remembered thinking: "Now what did we do that for? Ain't they mad enough at us already?"

Max Leslie's seventeen dive bombers were still circling over *Yorktown* at 12:07 P.M., when their pilots heard an imperative order: "All planes, get clear! The ship is about to be attacked!" The dive bombers moved out of the land-ing pattern and outside the range of *Yorktown*'s guns.

Yorktown put up twelve Wildcats to engage the attack-ing Japanese; they were piloted by Scotty McCuskey, Bill Woollen, Harry Gibbs, Dick Wright, Art Brassfield, Bill Barnes, Ed Mattson, D. C. ("Daddy") Barnes, Dick Crom-melin, J. B. Bain, D. C. Sheedy, and H. A. Bass. One six-plane division was led by Crommelin; the other by Brass-field. Joining them were several Wildcats rushed to *York-town* from *Hornet*. Before they took on the Japanese, the *Hornet* fighters made firing runs against Leslie's dive bombers; luckily, the *Hornet* planes missed.

The twenty-four Japanese planes—eighteen dive bomb-ers and six Zeros led by Lieutenant Michio Kobayashi—arrived over the target at 12:10 P.M., drawn to *Yorktown* by the guiding radio beam from *Tone*'s snooping float plane. Commander Chauncey Crutcher, executive officer of the cruiser *Astoria*, watched the enemy squadron as it flew into a cloud bank. "Immediately after they had disappeared into the clouds," he wrote after the battle, "six of them were observed to fall from the clouds and crash into the sea in flames."

Yorktown's Wildcats, although outnumbered two to one, were giving everything they had. "We broke radio silence," recalled Lieutenant Ed Mattson, "because it had no further significance once the Japanese had us in sight. It was a scramble for altitude for those of us just launched. Our planes were never noted for their ability to climb, and we just made it."

A Zero caught Mattson from behind and began pumping slugs into his right wing. Mattson's wingman, Ensign Bass, came tearing in and plucked off the Zero with a burst from his machine guns. Seconds later, Mattson encountered a Val dive bomber nose to nose. The Val pushed over to get under Mattson's fire. Mattson rolled over and got the Japanese plane in his sights again. He was pouring bullets into its front cockpit when he noticed that the rear gunner had his canopy closed, his 7.7-millimeter machine gun still immobile in the locked position. Mattson's bullets moved back and into the rear cockpit. "I could clearly see the bright orange tracers pouring through the shattered cockpit and into his body," Mattson reported. "It made me slightly sick." As Mattson pulled into a climbing turn, he and Bass, his wingman, saw the Val dive vertically into the ocean. The two pilots then began to look for new targets, but all the Japanese planes had passed them by. "Air action," noted Mattson, "is fast."

Other *Yorktown* pilots were scoring, too. Scotty Mc-Cuskey, one of *Yorktown's* original heroes (for shooting down a Japanese plane, a Kawanishi flying boat, so long ago), trailed Bill Woollen and Daddy Barnes in a rush against the Japanese formation. Harry Gibbs, a little farther behind, was McCuskey's wingman.

Woollen and Barnes were the first to open fire, but they both must have missed, for McCuskey saw no planes fall from the enemy formation. Then it was his turn. "The dive bombers," he reported, "were flying in a V of V's, and there were eighteen of them, the fixed landing gear Vals." He and Gibbs came in from the left of the Japanese squadron. One V was to McCuskey's left; another was to his right, much closer; and the third V was farther away, but almost straight ahead. "I went straight through the first V and took the outside man." McCuskey shot that plane down and then turned slightly to his right, aiming for three other Japanese planes. "I swung right across, and I mean I was looking them right in the eye." He nailed the two rear Japanese planes in the second V and kept right on going. From then on, he stated, "it was just shooting from the hip, and I found myself in the damndest dogfight you ever saw. I ended up with two of those Vals right on my tail."

McCuskey put his Wildcat into a deep-dive spiral to get away from the two dive bombers. When he started to climb for altitude, he found that he was out of ammunition. He began to swear at the plane that someone had believed to be an improved version of the Wildcat he had flown at the Coral Sea. The old F4F-3 was a four-gun fighter, 450 rounds for each gun. The new F4F-4 was one of those which, with two additional machine guns, carried less ammunition per gun. As if that were not bad enough, the old Wildcat, it suddenly seemed to McCuskey (and to some of the other pilots), had been more maneuverable than the new one.

McCuskey informed *Yorktown* by radio that he was coming in for more ammunition; the carrier instructed him to hold off. Then McCuskey found himself on the tail of another Japanese bomber; it would have been a sure kill if he had had some ammunition. "Then I remembered that Thach had told us, 'When you run out of ammunition, chop their tails off!' We'd heard that the Germans or someone did this." McCuskey actually tried. He swung from one side to the other of the Val, only feet from its tail; the Val's rear gunner swung his weapon back and forth, too, in metronomic time. It was then that McCuskey began to have doubts about this system. "If I chop this guy's tail off with my propeller," he recalled saying to himself, "I won't even have time to get out of this airplane. So I decided to give that idea up for the day."

Commander Crutcher of *Astoria* watched as the Japanese planes emerged from the clouds. "They were still being attacked by our planes," he wrote.

All the *Yorktown* pilots, with the exception of Harry Gibbs and Dick Wright, got at least one enemy plane. A number of the kills, however, were listed as probables because *Hornet*'s fighters also claimed some successes. *Yorktown*'s Art Brassfield—"the teacher and steadying influence among us young ensigns," according to one Fighting 42 pilot, and "beyond all question the best damned pilot in the squadron," according to another—shot down three dive bombers, including one that was trying to strafe a downed *Yorktown* torpedo plane. Barnes, Haas, Mattson, and Bass were credited with a dive bomber apiece. Crommelin, Bain, and Sheedy were credited with a Zero apiece.

When Lieutenant Kobayashi's squadron finally came into range of Task Force 17's guns, its strength had been whittled from eighteen dive bombers and six fighters to eight bombers and three fighters. Thirteen planes had been shot down. More, perhaps many more, would have been destroyed, had *Yorktown's* fighters been able to fire more rounds.

It was May 8 at the Coral Sea all over again. *Yorktown's* attack planes had struck the enemy surface force hard. Her defending aviators had performed magnificently against superior numbers. This time the Japanese carriers had started the day with 272 fighters, dive bombers, and torpedo planes. Of all these airplanes, only 11 were now close enough to attack one American aircraft carrier. And of those 11 planes, only 8—fixed landing gear Vals—carried striking power: eight 550-pound bombs.

Chapter Thirteen

★ ★ ★ ★ ★ ★ ★

★ ★ ★ Eight Japanese Vals, their tops a muddy brown, their bottoms silver, and their tails a gleaming yellow, plunged down at *Yorktown* at a dive angle of seventy degrees. They came in from the carrier's port side, abaft the beam, smart tactically because both heavy-gunned cruisers were positioned on *Yorktown's* starboard.

Yorktown had been through this sort of thing before, and she was ready. Every gun on the ship, including a number of Springfield rifles distributed to the mess stewards, was turned toward the attackers.

Telephone talkers gave and relayed instructions. Musician Frank Thompson was at Repair 4, in *Yorktown's* galley, hooked in with Musician Hank Fogle on the bridge. Water Tender Frank Luckiesh had the smoke watch up in the stack, just as he had had it at the Coral Sea. Both Lieutenants Norwood Campbell and John Preston, *Yorktown's* landing signal officers, were at their station on the LSO platform when the Japanese attack began. Preston, remembering Captain Buckmaster's caution that the two men should separate during battle so that they would not be killed together, turned to Campbell and said, "So long, Soupy, I'll see you later." Then he started forward along the flight deck.

Yorktowners, in fact, were surprisingly calm. "We were blooded and confident," recalled Lieutenant (jg) Harry Glick, who commanded the five-inch guns aft on *Yorktown*'s starboard catwalk.

Once *Yorktown*'s Wildcats had peeled away, their ammunition spent, the carrier's gunners opened up on the Vals. The sky was soon filled with black puffs, and Lieutenant Commander Ernie Davis' voice again came booming over the loudspeakers: "Air department take cover! Gunnery department take over!"

It is hard to say who scored, for both *Yorktown* and the portside destroyers were firing, and then the cruisers and the destroyers on the starboard side joined in. Two of the Vals, however, were nailed on the way down. The plane piloted by Lieutenant Kobayashi, leader of the strike, disintegrated in midair. His pilots were well trained, rigidly disciplined; they kept coming on.

All six remaining planes dropped their bombs. One of the Vals was destroyed as he pulled out. Seaman Rudy Yirok, manning a .30-caliber machine gun just aft of *Yorktown*'s island, claimed a piece of him. "I put nearly two hundred rounds into that plane," Yirok said, "and was so excited by the time he went into the sea that I swallowed my chew of tobacco."

Ensign Harvey Lasell, who earlier had done well in directing his five-inch fire at the Coral Sea, had trouble this time. "Smoke from the stack and from gunfire obscured the visibility of my director." Lasell reported that Lloyd Rice, who controlled the elevation sights, suddenly cried, "I can't see!"

Yorktown's fantail, at the time the attack began, was about one-third covered with wooden trash. A warship, in a time of action, rarely burns trash at sea for fear that its incinerator smoke will reveal her position. Nor is the trash thrown overboard, lest it give enemy submarines a direct trail to follow. Seaman Bill Federowicz, the man in charge of the trash, was under orders to throw it over the side only when battle was joined. But as the Vals began their attack, the trash was still sitting there on the fantail. "I was told that all those guys with battle stations on the fantail were supposed to help me, but no one did," Federowicz wrote, "so I stopped heaving the stuff over." He had, in fact, left the trash to help man a gun. He was removing an empty ammunition magazine from it when a Japanese near-miss exploded just off Yorktown's stern.

"Shrapnel from that miss killed men near me," according to Federowicz, "and it cut some of the lifelines. That made a bunch of our antisplinter mats fall over the side. A couple of pieces also started a fire in the stack of crates; some punctured a barrel of aviation lube oil, and some knocked a lot of holes in the bulkhead between us and the hangar deck. When I saw smoke coming from that pile of boxes, I yelled and got everyone to help me throw them overboard. Pretty soon there was a long line of boxes drifting astern."

Three near-misses lifted Yorktown's stern clear of the water, and the violent spinning of her screws made her tail shimmy. Seaman Ed Cavanaugh was at his .50-caliber machine gun below the landing signal officer's platform. Fragments from a portside near-miss took a leg off his loader, lacerated the soles of another man's feet, and punctured Cavanaugh in twenty-two places. His left hand shattered, Cavanaugh tried to get across the flight deck for help. As he staggered across the deck, he was hit three more times by slugs from a dive bomber's machine guns. By the time a corpsman got him to sick bay, Cavanaugh was bleeding from a hand, both arms, a knee, and a hip.

On *Yorktown's* bridge, Paul Kroll, Wally Whalen, and Charles Thomas were blazing away with .50-caliber machine guns Lieutenant Commander Ernie Davis had reluctantly turned over to them after the Coral Sea. Each gun had a wooden plug to seal its water jacket. When the guns overheated, as they were now doing, the plugs popped out like champagne corks. Each time it happened, someone would grab a coffeepot full of water, refill the sizzling jacket, and hammer the plug back in. The guns, sizzling and popping, never stopped firing for very long.

Captain Buckmaster, racing *Yorktown* through her paces again, managed to evade three Japanese bombs. The carrier was turning and twisting at thirty knots. "It felt like we were inside a cocktail shaker," Storekeeper Tom Callaghan reported.

The Japanese pilots kept on coming against all this firepower. They were doing just what Jo-Jo Powers had done at the Coral Sea—flying in so close that they could almost lay their bombs right on the carrier's deck. Ensign Harvey Lasell saw all three of the bombs that hit. The first one barely missed him.

"I watched that bomb," he said later. "It was heading

straight for our director (a computer-connected firing device). Its line didn't move a bit to either side. In those few seconds I thought of all the wonderful things there were to experience in this life, and I had a sense of utter regret that I wasn't going to live to enjoy them."

Lasell and Fire Controlman Charles Tyson exchanged glances, and then they shook hands. "See you in hell," said Tyson. Just then *Yorktown* lurched to starboard from the shock of a near-miss on her port quarter, and the bomb Lasell had been watching "went right by us, inboard. It pierced the flight deck at the base of the island structure, directly in line with the foot of the director. It had passed within ten feet of us."

The second bomb struck *Yorktown*'s flight deck about fifty feet aft of Ensign Lasell's gun mount. "I had my helmet on," Lasell reported, "and I was standing up, so my head just cleared the top of our splinter shield. Suddenly I felt as though I had been hit in the side of my head with a sledgehammer. My right ear was numb." When someone told Lasell that he was wounded, he touched the right side of his head and felt blood streaming down it. A minute or two later he heard someone asking his telephone talker if he were dead. "Our report," said Lasell, "was negative."

Lasell's guns, had they been able to fire accurately through the smoke, might have been able to get the third plane that had scored the hit, for it had made its approach directly in line with the five-inchers. It laid its bomb on *Yorktown*'s forward elevator.

Printer Jimmy Mertens was mesmerized by one of the dive bombers. He stood on the flight deck and watched it come straight at him. "It looked like a speck up there in the sky," he said later. "Then he got bigger and bigger as he came down." Mertens finally realized his own peril and dived headfirst down a short ladder. "I landed on a bunch of guys who had outguessed me." Then the bomb exploded.

The man underneath Mertens had both legs almost blown away. The man on top of Mertens, the last to dive down the ladder, had shrapnel in his side. Mertens crawled back up the ladder to a terrible scene. The ladder was next to the 1.1-inch guns. "I could see that the entire crew of the guns had literally been blown to pieces. Arms and legs and parts of bodies were lying around inside the shield of each mount. All the blood I found on me was that of my shipmates." The bomb, which had detonated on impact, exploded inboard of the guns, and its concussion had caught the gunners inside the antisplinter shield.

Ensign John Lorenz, in charge of the two after 1.1-inch mounts, was knocked unconscious. When he later came to, his eyes met a sight forever to remain with him. A score of the men with whom he had spent so many nights and days on watch were dead, parts of their bodies scattered about. In one trainer's seat rested the hips and legs of a man. The rest of him had disappeared.

Chief Gunner's Mate Albert Noland reacted from long training. He soon had cooks, musicians, and seamen up from belowdecks. They removed the bodies and parts of bodies of those killed and took their places. It was not long before the guns were again ready for action.

Seaman Tony Blazaukas was manning a machine gun just forward of the 1.1-inch mounts. The blast killed his loader and blew him, dazed but otherwise unhurt, into an ammunition loading room. Working near Blazaukas were Gunner's Mates Ted Metcalf and Jack Magan. Metcalf was blown into a clipping room, where bullets were loaded on belts. When he staggered outside, he almost stepped on Magan's dead body. The two men had been standing almost shoulder to shoulder.

Chief Milt Wester of Fighting 42 (now 3) was at a fire-fighting station on *Yorktown's* hangar deck. Most of his own planes were in the air, and Wester had been helping get seven dive bombers ready for an attack. The seven planes were loaded and fueled and parked in the after end of the hangar deck. Then the bomb that had wiped out the 1.1 gun crews came blasting through the overhead into the hangar deck. "The bomb," reported Wester, "had some kind of phosphorous content, and this sprayed over some of the planes. They caught fire. Being loaded and fueled, they were in danger of exploding. There were also live bombs and torpedoes on the hangar deck. Water wouldn't put the fire out, so the danger was terrific. I had my crew chop the burning wing off one plane, so the fire wouldn't reach its fuel tanks."

When the fires broke out, Lieutenant Ace Emerson turned on all the sprinkler systems. The hangar deck was divided into four giant bays; the sprinklers dropped curtains of water across the ship's width, isolating each bay. By his quick action, Emerson confined the fire to Bay Number 4, and fire-fighting teams eventually put it out.

Seaman Carl Tyler, a crewman of Torpedo 5 kept aboard to service planes of Torpedo 3, was wounded by the blast. "I was wearing one of those World War I soup plate helmets," he reported, "and I was flattened out on the deck when the blast came. I saw a bright flash of fire and heard the explosions and then felt a sharp pain in my hip. My helmet was stripped from my head, although I had a strap under my chin. I saw the helmet go clattering away, down the deck, aft. My left leg began to go numb, so I reached back to see if I had one. I wished I hadn't. There was a gaping hole in the hip, and when I looked around, I could see blood running out on the deck. I rolled over and tried to get up. That's when I saw two SBD's on fire, not forty feet from me. That helped me get up, believe me!"

Tyler hobbled toward two friends, seeking assistance. But both of them were in shock, too frightened to move. Dazed, Tyler staggered to *Yorktown's* port side and looked out through an opening. "That's when I got clobbered again, with a hit in my right shoulder blade." He was knocked down, to be picked up later by someone and carried to sick bay. Medics found a piece of steel sticking half an inch out of his shoulder. "The doctor poured some kind of red fluid on my wounds, and—wow!—I bet I smoked for five minutes." Corpsmen then removed Tyler's clothing, promising him they would bring some pajamas later. They never did; Tyler went through the rest of the battle naked.

The first bomb had killed and maimed, but it had not impaired *Yorktown's* fighting ability. The 1.1.-inch guns were operating again, minutes after the blast. And the great ship was still steaming at thirty knots.

It was another bomb that seriously hurt *Yorktown*, although it killed no one. This one came down on a port-to-starboard slant, punctured the flight deck, and exploded in the uptakes from *Yorktown*'s firerooms. It was, in effect, a pilot's dream—a down-the-stack shot.

"The most serious effect of this bomb hit," wrote Captain Buckmaster in his action report, "was that it ruptured the uptakes from Boilers 1, 2, and 3; completely disabled Boilers 2 and 3, and extinguished fires in Boilers 2, 3, 4, 5, and 6."

Steam was the giant that powered *Yorktown*. The steam came from water in the boilers, heated by the intense fuel fires. Smoke from these fires was carried away through uptakes that led ultimately to *Yorktown*'s stacks—her chimneys—which were enclosed in her superstructure. Three of *Yorktown*'s boilers, the superheaters that gave an extra push to her turbines, had not been repaired at Pearl Harbor, so that they were not operating at all. Of the six remaining boilers, five had been blown out by the Japanese bomb. Without the boilers, *Yorktown* could not move.

When a 20,000-ton warship making thirty knots starts to lose way, it can be felt all over the ship. The decks, the overheads, and the bulkheads vibrate first at lesser frequencies and finally not at all. Eight minutes after this bomb struck *Yorktown*, she was helpless. There was no power to work her guns, no power to run her elevators. Even the motor powering the gyrocompass slowed down, and the wheel on the bridge was useless.

The third bomb pierced *Yorktown*'s forward elevator and rammed deeply—as deeply as the bomb that had done the damage at the Coral Sea. It exploded in a room set aside for the storage of bales of rags in the forward part of the ship. Only a handful of men were at battle stations in that section, and no one was killed. A small hole the bomb left in the flight deck was quickly patched with boiler plate.

But with all those rags to feed it, a troublesome fire broke out. Worse, the rag room was close to ammunition magazines and a compartment full of high-octane gasoline. If the ammunition and the fuel were set off, the entire forward section of the ship would be blown away. That might have happened, except for the fact that Lieutenant Emerson, only minutes earlier, had spread a blanket of carbon dioxide around the gasoline storage space. Then, too, Chief Gunner's Mate Vardie Taylor was quick-witted: after figuring out where the fire was located, he turned a valve and flooded the ammunition magazines with seawater. The danger from fire was averted, but the fire in the rag room burned on. Because of choking smoke, the rag room could be approached only through one compartment, and it was accessible only through one of the narrow chimneylike trunks that rise vertically through certain sections of a warship.

Commander Dixie Kiefer was ordered by Buckmaster to assess the damage. He looked things over, turned to the members of the repair party, and said, "Well, boys, the only thing for us to do is run this hose down that trunk and get at it." He pointed at the trunk opening, from which smoke was drifting.

Humor never deserts some men, no matter what the circumstance, and a sailor standing between the commander and the hatch leaped gracefully aside, bowed, and swept an arm toward the opening. "After you, Commander," he said. Kiefer grinned, swung the nozzle of the hose over his shoulder, and started down the trunk. The sailor followed him.

If *Yorktown* were to be saved, it would have to be done below in the firerooms, where the real damage was and where the real battle now began. When the bomb blew out five of *Yorktown*'s six boilers, it also blasted stack gas back into all the firerooms. Only one who has grappled with stack gas can appreciate its ghastly qualities. Once in a man's eyes, it cannot be rubbed out; the particles are too big. It must be sluiced out or removed with a cotton swab. Inhaling stack gas is like sucking in fire; it parches the throat and sears the stomach. Because of the gas, *Yorktown*'s firerooms had to be evacuated, all except Fire Room 1, where Water Tender Charles Kleinsmith was boss. Boiler 1 was the only boiler that had survived the explosion, but gas was seeping into the fire room, and Kleinsmith and his men—Water Tender Cliff Snell and Firemen Earl Jansen, Roy Ellison, Jim Benton, Bill Brewer, and Cecil Brooks—were ordered to evacuate.

The crew was just leaving when Kleinsmith bellowed, "Where the hell do you think you're going? They're going to need this boiler!"

Even though the boiler was red-hot, its insulating brick was knocked away, and fuel registering 180 degrees Fahrenheit was spitting from damaged oil heaters, Kleinsmith's men turned to with a will—perhaps with too much of a will. They began working Boiler 1 so fast that smoke from it was sucked into other firerooms. Lieutenant Reed Cundiff, the boiler officer, had to pass word to hold it down a little. Kleinsmith's crew eased the steam pressure a bit—a very little bit.

Boiler 1, even at its low level of output, was producing enough electric power to run *Yorktown*'s auxiliary machinery. Blowers, ever so slowly, removed stack gas from the other firerooms. After a while, other gangs were able to return to their posts. By itself, Kleinsmith's crew kept things going until 1:20 P.M., an hour after *Yorktown* had stopped dead in the water. Number 4 boiler was cut back in; the fires were restarted under 5 and 6.

At 1:50 P.M., his sweaty face broken by a grin, Commander Delaney called the bridge. "Captain," he said, "the engine room reports ready to make twenty knots or better."

Buckmaster acknowledged the message crisply. "Very well," he said. It had been all of that—and more.

Topside, Yorktowners tended the wounded and carried away the dead. The living shook hands with one another. Seaman Tom Edwards, near Gun 7, especially congratulated a machine gunner. The gunner, whose issue dungarees had worn out long ago, had been given a pair of pants contrived from canvas sailcloth by Boatswain's Mate John Sharp. The crotch in the pants went all the way down to the gunner's knees. Edwards noted that a bullet had passed cleanly through the canvas, between the gunner's knees.

Inside *Yorktown*'s bridge structure Seaman Warren Woodard was torn by indecision. He watched as Chief Signalman Demps Gordy and Ensign Harvey Vogel clawed frantically at a raincoat locker, from which they had seen what they thought was blood dripping to the deck. Gordy and Vogel assumed that someone, in fright, had hidden in the locker and had been hit badly. Seaman Woodard knew better. He and some friends had "liberated" three gallons of tomato juice at Pearl Harbor and had stored it in the locker. He decided to allow the two men to break open the locker and discover the truth for themselves.

Other Yorktowners went to work patching a large hole in the flight deck. Timbers were placed on exposed girders, and then smaller timbers were placed on them. In this way, wooden braces were built up to a level with the deck. Boiler plates were then laid over the timber and secured in place with railroad spikes to match the flat deck surface. The hole in the forward elevator, being small—for the bomb that had made it was of the delayed-action type— was quickly repaired.

At the point when *Yorktown* had been dead in the water, without radio and without radar, Admiral Fletcher had come to a reluctant decision. Without proper communications facilities, he could not command, and he had no choice but to transfer, with his staff, to another ship. *Yorktown* sent a signal to *Astoria*, which lowered a boat, and shortly after 12:40 P.M. the admiral and his staff climbed aboard the cruiser. Also coming aboard *Astoria* were two *Yorktown* pilots, Max Leslie and Swede Holmberg, who had ditched their planes after they had run out of gas and been picked up by a whaleboat from the cruiser.

Yorktown's other planes were taken in by *Hornet* and *Enterprise*. In a tragic accident the wounded pilot of a *Yorktown* Wildcat landed on *Hornet* without turning off his gun switch. The shock of the landing activated his guns, spraying the carrier's superstructure and killing a number of men, among them Lieutenant Royal Ingersoll, the son of an admiral.

The Japanese were also working. Admiral Yamamoto was still hundreds of miles away, his flag in the battleship *Yamato*. The news he had received from Nagumo was desperate, and at 12:20 P.M. he decided that he would have to commit his surface ships if the battle were to be won. He then radioed his northern force, off the Aleutians, and ordered its two carriers to make all speed for Midway. Next, he directed the commander of his invasion force to send the transports to the northwest, out of harm's way, and to rush his heavy cruisers to Midway.

Yamamoto intended to hit Midway with the four heavy cruisers from the invasion convoy. First, however, the submarine *I-168*, still prowling off the island, would have the honor of firing the opening shot from her four-inch deck gun. At about 2:30 A.M. on the following morning, a surface attack on Midway would begin. The island would be flattened; all danger of air attack from that quarter would be removed. Then, if his capital ships could catch up with the American fleet, it, too, would be destroyed.

At 2 P.M., *Yorktown* got under way again. No longer burning, she resumed the fueling of her on-deck fighters. By 2:17 P.M. she was making almost seventeen knots, and her escorts had once again surrounded her in Cruising Disposition Victor. Nine minutes later *Astoria's* radar picked up a second Japanese strike from the carrier *Hiryu*, just thirty-three miles away, winging straight for *Yorktown*. This low-flying attack, like the first, had come in under *Yorktown's* straight-line radar beam, demonstrating that the Japanese, too, had benefited from the experiences of the preceding battles.

Chapter Fourteen

★ ★ ★ ★ ★ ★ ★

★ ★ ★ It seemed hardly fair. No American warship had ever before been attacked so often or so hard. Now driving toward *Yorktown* were sixteen Japanese planes led by a gallant fighter, Lieutenant Joichi Tomonaga, who had taken off from *Hiryu* fully aware that one of his fuel tanks had been damaged in the earlier attack on Midway and that he would never return to his ship. He had only enough gas for a one-way trip.

Later in the war an attack such as Tomonaga's would have been chewed apart miles from its target, but not now, in spite of the fact that *Yorktown* and the other American ships with her had both the planes and the firepower to fend off their attackers. Orbiting over the carrier were six of her own Wildcats, three from *Enterprise*, and three more of her own that had taken off from *Enterprise*.

One of the Yorktowners from *Enterprise* was the intrepid Scotty McCuskey. "We were given a vector," he stated, "and we went out on it. But in those days radar couldn't tell you the height of the incoming aircraft. We naturally figured it was a high-altitude flight, and so we started climbing. Well, those so-and-so's slipped in beneath us. That could have been my day all right, if we hadn't missed those torpedo planes. With Bill Woollen and Harry Gibbs, with my four planes, and with what Thach brought up, we had enough to do the job." Unable to find the enemy, McCuskey and three *Enterprise* planes had to put about and return to their carriers.

Ten other Wildcats were among the planes being refueled on *Yorktown's* deck when *Astoria's* radar first picked up the Japanese strike. With another attack imminent, refueling had to be canceled and fuel lines drained and filled again with carbon dioxide. Four of the ten fighters, piloted by John Thach, Bill Leonard, John Adams, and G. F. Hopper, roared off. All had less than twenty-five gallons of gasoline in their tanks. Technically at least, *Yorktown* had a fighter cover of sixteen planes—one fighter for each enemy plane. The odds, on paper, were even for a change.

At 2:26 P.M., Lieutenant Tomonaga instructed his fliers to deploy for attack. Four minutes later, *Yorktown* lookouts spotted the Nakajimas, nine miles to the west. At 2:33 P.M., Tomonaga shouted into his microphone, "All planes, go in!" The Japanese planes, in beginning their attack, ran through a cloud formation. The quartermaster of the watch on board *Astoria* noted in the ship's log that four enemy planes were observed falling out of the clouds in flames.

One of them was probably Bill Woollen's victim. "I was at about seven thousand feet when I spotted a torpedo plane ahead of me and below me," Woollen reported. "I overtook him and shot him down at about four thousand feet. After watching him spin, I went straight ahead for a few moments, and then I felt a heavy jolt in my left wing.

I looked out, to see oil from the cooler in that wing spilling out."

Woollen knew that he had only a few minutes left before the engine overheated and cut out. "My first thoughts were to get out of there before I got hit again. I never did see the guy who got me. I noticed that Yorktown was heading into the wind, so I figured my best bet would be to land as far ahead of the task force as possible, where the ships would pass me by and lend a hand." Woollen ditched about five miles ahead of Yorktown and was picked up by a destroyer.

Because Yorktown planes and pilots had been scattered among three ships, records of their performance are confused. But Woollen got one plane; Thach claimed a torpedo plane, as did Bill Leonard and John Adams.

Adams, one of the four pilots who took off from Yorktown short of fuel just as the Japanese began their attack, stated, "By the time I was launched, our ship's guns were blasting. I never will forget trying to roll up my wheels, charge my guns, and get my plane sighted in on a torpedo plane, all at the same time." He hit one Nakajima before it could drop its torpedo, poured slugs into another that had already dropped its torpedo, and suddenly found that he was in the middle of the Japanese formation, under a hail of fire from the Japanese and from the cruisers, destroyers, and Yorktown. "One of the destroyers seemed to have it in for me. He kept firing at me long after the attack was over. I can't remember which one it was, but my buddy Dick Crommelin nearly got into a fight with its gunnery officer in Hawaii a week later."

Ensign Melvin Tootle, like Adams, was forced to take off

from *Yorktown* in haste. He had barely cleared *Yorktown's* bow when he made a violent turn to engage an incoming enemy torpedo plane; he began firing almost before his wheels were up. His ejected .50-caliber shells rattled like hailstones on the decks of the destroyer *Balch*. Then he was hit, perhaps by the Japanese, more likely by the Americans. He pulled his Wildcat into a half-loop and radioed that he was bailing out. Tootle, who was picked up later, still holds the world record for short-duration combat: he was in the air for only thirty seconds.

By 2:40 P.M. *Yorktown's* fighters could do nothing more to forestall the attack, for the Japanese were in range of American surface gunfire. To pursue the enemy into that holocaust would be suicidal. *Yorktown* pilots, after the battle, reported that they had downed seven enemy planes; the records, however, are imperfect. This much is clear: six of the ten Japanese torpedo planes were able to get close enough to launch their missiles at *Yorktown*.

Sharp gunnery from the defending ships might have brought them all down, but the shooting was poor. Gunnery doctrine in mid-1942 was crude compared with the art it had become by V-J Day. In the early stages of the Pacific war, guns were not radar-directed and the proximity fuze, to become so deadly later, was still only a laboratory project. *Yorktown* and her consorts did the best they could with barrage fire, in which fuzes were set to explode at a predetermined distance from the defending ships. The guns kept firing at a fixed range until enemy planes flew into their bursts or until the fuzes were reset. But *Yorktown*, having been worked up to 20.5 knots and dodging frantically once again, was a difficult platform from which to direct gunfire. The escorting ships had to keep station on her, and this made accuracy difficult for their pointers and trainers. Too, the Japanese came in very low, so that a fast-moving cruiser or destroyer sometimes blocked the firing path of another ship. Again, the unexpectedly high speed of the Japanese torpedo planes led gunnery officers astray because ranges closed much faster than they had estimated, so that gunbursts appeared behind the attackers. Deflection as well was off because the gunners were estimating the speed of the Nakajimas at 125 to 130 knots, when they actually were making closer to 180 knots. As a result, the gunners failed to lead their targets enough.

Mack Helmerich of Bombing 5 was at his fire-fighting station on the hangar deck. "I saw one flight of three Japanese planes come in," he recalled. "Only one of them got his fish away. The other two were knocked down before they could release. Out of a second flight of three planes, two got their fish away." Helmerich watched the torpedoes head for *Yorktown*'s port side. He lined up their trajectory and then ducked for shelter as far away from the estimated point of impact as he could get.

Two groups of Japanese planes tried to cross over *Yorktown* and attack her from the starboard side, in a maneuver the reverse of that which Torpedo 3 had attempted earlier against *Hiryu*. The two groups never made it, but four or perhaps five Japanese torpedo planes were able to launch their torpedoes with a chance of scoring; all of them attacked from the port side. As soon as their torpedoes hit the water, Captain Buckmaster spun *Yorktown* into a hard left turn. He intended to comb the torpedo tracks—that is, run between them—as he had done successfully at the Coral Sea.

This time success was only partial. Buckmaster managed to evade one torpedo; it passed astern. Another missed to port. Both of them had been released by the planes attacking from the sternmost position. Two other Nakajima pilots attacked from farther ahead, one coming to within 500 yards of *Yorktown* before he let his torpedo go.

At 2:41 P.M. every man aboard *Yorktown* felt the ship lurch to starboard, then shudder violently. Two torpedoes crashed into her port side, less than sixty feet apart. An immense puff of white smoke gushed from her stacks as she swung left. She continued to swing in a tight circle, listed sharply to port, and stopped dead in the water.

There are only two ways in which a major warship like *Yorktown* could be badly hurt. One was to put a bomb down her stacks, knocking out her power plant, which the Japanese had done earlier, on June 4, only to be foiled by the heroic efforts of Bill Kleinsmith and his helpers in Fire Room 1. The second was to put a torpedo into the ship's firerooms, which would also knock out the power plant, perhaps even open up a hole large enough for tons of seawater to pour in and drag the ship to the bottom.

The Japanese, in a combination of skill and courage, had managed to put not one but two torpedoes into *Yorktown's* firerooms. The first burst through the fuel tanks outboard of Fire Rooms 2 and 6, close to the bulkhead that separated them, then exploded. These two immense rooms, each nearly the size of a three-story house, were blown apart. The intervening bulkhead was shattered, and seawater rushed in to fill the void.

The second torpedo hit forward of Fire Room 2, in a generator room. All hands in the room must have been killed instantly.

Yorktown now lay open to the sea for some sixty-five feet along her port side. Tons of water streamed in, and she began to lean heavily to her port side where the weight of the water was concentrated. For a few seconds it appeared that she would roll over on her left side or capsize.

The fires under all her boilers were extinguished as water poured into the firerooms on the port side and resulting concussion blew out fires on the starboard side. Her entire power output was shut down; her four screws slowed and then stopped. The rudder was jammed fifteen degrees to the left. For the second time in 155 minutes Yorktown was completely helpless.

This time Kleinsmith and his gang would not be around to save her. After the dive bomber attack, he and his men had staggered, sooty-black and exhausted, to the post office compartment, where they had dropped in their tracks. This compartment was directly above the explosion of the first torpedo. Kleinsmith and his gang, along with two telephone talkers from the ship's band, Musicians Gordon Roop and John Seymour, were killed instantly.

Water Tender George Handford and his gang, stationed in a fireroom other than Kleinsmith's, had also gone to the post office compartment for a brief rest. Like all below-decks men, they rested at the ready, prepared to move wherever needed. Handford, memories of Repair 5's fate at the Coral Sea fresh in his mind, decided that the compartment was too crowded. He took his men into the adjoining compartment aft and closed the watertight door behind him. Minutes later the torpedo struck *Yorktown*. Handford and the three men with him were not scratched.

The two blasts were stunning. *Yorktown* rolled over to thirty degrees as water lapped at her hangar deck. She faltered, then eased back, settling in at a twenty-six-degree angle.

Reports came funneling into the bridge. Commander Delaney's was one of the first. "All boiler fires are out, Captain," he told Buckmaster. Ernie Davis reported that all his gunners were still at their stations, despite the ship's wild extreme inclination. Manual controls would have to be used to fire the guns, he explained, but it could be done.

Other reports came in.

"Fire Rooms Two and Six flooded."

"Forward generator room flooded. Crew does not acknowledge transmissions. Think they're all dead."

"Leaks in Fire Rooms One and Four. Shipping water."

"All power lost."

"After emergency diesel generator operating, but she keeps cutting out." (This emergency system, running on diesel fuel, was hardly enough to sustain lighting.)

"Damage incurred in sick bay. We've got to get the wounded out of there quick."

"Switchboard destroyed."

At this point Buckmaster could not have distributed electric power throughout his ship had it been available to him.

Capping all the discouraging news was that from Lieutenant Commander Clarence Aldrich, the ship's damage control officer. It was his duty to assess the damage and to direct the attempt to repair it.

If *Yorktown* were to fight again in this battle, even to

try to get away, she had somehow to be brought back to an even keel so that her boiler fires could be relighted. To right her, those compartments now open to the sea must be sealed off, then pumps put to work, sucking water from spaces made secure against the sea. Some of the pumps would drain this water over the side; others would shift it into empty starboard fuel and ballast tanks to increase the ship's weight on that side. Still others would be needed to transfer hundreds of tons of fuel oil from port to starboard to serve as a counterweight. Chief George Vavrek, the "oil king," was intimately familiar with the ship's maze of pipes, lines, valves, tanks, and fuel storage spaces, and he knew how to do the job. But there was one drawback, as Aldrich explained to Captain Buckmaster: "Without power to the pumps, I see no hope of correcting this list."

The ship's listing was frighteningly erratic. It would first increase, then ease back, then increase again. No one could be sure just what might happen next.

Captain Buckmaster conferred with his department heads as he tried to analyze the ship's condition objectively. He could not right the ship in order to light off the boilers without power, and power would come only from functioning boilers. Second, although the ship's guns were manned, tilted at a twenty-six-degree angle, they were unable to hit anything. Third, the ship might roll over on her beam ends at any moment, taking most of the crew to the bottom with her. On the one hand, she *might* remain afloat —one of only three carriers opposing Japan's ambitions in the Pacific. On the other, more than 2,000 men, battle-tested, courageous, expert—

The decision was Buckmaster's alone. Admiral Fletcher was in the cruiser *Astoria*, but even had he still been aboard, the decision would have been Buckmaster's. At 2:58 P.M. the captain turned to Dixie Kiefer, his executive officer, and gave the fateful order: "Pass the word to abandon ship."

Men who have never borne the weight of command have derided Buckmaster for this decision, pointing out that *Yorktown*, after all, did not sink. That fact is irrefutable, *now*. Buckmaster listened to the expert advice that was available to him, he weighed alternatives, and he concluded that *Yorktown* was in danger of sinking. No man who was aboard *Yorktown* that day disagreed. The ship, by all objective analysis, was in danger of sinking.

From the bridge of *Astoria*, Fletcher saw what was happening. He supported Buckmaster's decision, and he later reported to Admiral Nimitz that he had done so.

Orders to abandon ship were passed by word of mouth. When they got to *Yorktown's* main engine room, where no one had been killed or wounded, Commander Delaney said, "O.K., boys, up you go." The only way out was through an escape trunk, in which the ladder was on the starboard side. With *Yorktown* tilted so sharply to port, climbing the ladder was almost like trying to crawl across a ceiling.

Although the abandon-ship order had been passed, Rex Quillan, aviation mechanic in Scouting 5 and plane captain for Lieutenant (jg) C. N. Conatser's dive bomber, stepped up smartly to Commander Oscar Pederson and kept announcing, "Mister Conatser's plane is ready for takeoff, sir." His job was to help Conatser fight, and so far as he was concerned, the plane was ready despite the flight deck's cant.

The first man to leave *Yorktown* was Electrician's Mate Pete Newberg, blown through a hangar-deck opening when the torpedoes hit. Still told is the story that Chief Boatswain's Mate "Pop" Austin, *Yorktown*'s master-at-arms, leaned over the side and hollered, "Who gave you permission to depart this ship?"

Vane Bennett was not at all sure that he was going to be able to abandon ship. As he opened the door from the radar room, he was met by a wall of smoke and flame in the passageway. He ducked back inside and opened a port on the starboard side, pulled himself through, and slid down to the hangar deck. While Bennett stood there wondering what to do next, Bill Kelso, a boatswain's mate, edged up to him and said, "I've always wanted to dive off this flight deck. May I have permission to do so now?"

"Be my guest," said Bennett, half-joking. To his utter astonishment, Kelso poised at the deck's edge and then executed a graceful swan dive into the ocean seventy-five feet below.

What Tom Edwards remembered most vividly about abandoning *Yorktown* was the silence of the ship: "It was real eerie. You couldn't hear any of those blower sounds you usually hear on a ship or the creaking of the expansion joints. There was nothing except sort of shuffling sounds, as men headed for their abandon-ship stations."

Ship's Cook Tomas Saxon left *Yorktown* clutching the pet rabbit he had brought aboard at Pearl Harbor. Both nearly drowned when a sailor jumped into the water on top of them. Saxon's back was injured; complications developed, ultimately to prove fatal, and the rabbit outlived its master.

When everyone else had left the ship, Captain Buckmaster went over the side and grabbed hold of a raft loaded with wounded. The raft was being towed by a whaleboat to the destroyer *Hammann* when Buckmaster heard a cry for help. He looked around and saw a mess attendant thrashing wildly in the water. Buckmaster swam to the man and pulled him back to the raft. As Lieutenant Hurlbert later described the scene, "he looked like a great walrus, swimming along and holding the man's head out of the water."

Hundreds of pairs of shoes were lined up on *Yorktown*'s flight and hangar decks, in neat and orderly rows, as men prepared to abandon ship. The same thing had happened aboard *Lexington* when she had been abandoned at the Coral Sea. Much has been made of this, and the phenomenon is usually attributed to military discipline. Not so. As several Yorktowners have explained, "We saw some guys take off their shoes, so we did, too." It was as simple as that.

Lieutenant Hurlbert, who had watched his skipper rescue the mess attendant, eventually paddled alongside the destroyer *Benham*, where he grabbed the lines of a cargo net that had been draped over the side. He was just starting to climb aboard when he heard the destroyer's public-address system announce, "Stand by for enemy air attack!" It was a false alarm, one of several that occurred during the rescue of *Yorktown*'s crew, most of them touched off by the return of friendly planes.

"*Benham* was supposed to be the fastest ship in the Navy," Hurlbert noted. "The talk was that she had made forty-five knots in her sea trials when she was first built. Anyway, when that air-defense alarm sounded, she dug her old tail in and started to take off. I clutched at the cargo net automatically, of course. Before I could think of letting go, *Benham* was really picking up speed. With one arm poked through that cargo net, I didn't dare let go, for fear of getting caught in *Benham*'s screws. So there I was, flipping up and down on the wave tops as she dashed along. I'd hit, bounce up about ten feet, and then come back down with a mighty whap! Finally, on about my tenth bounce, someone reached out, grabbed me in midair, and pulled me aboard."

Most of *Yorktown*'s crew had been recovered by mid-afternoon, and all who were going to be rescued had been picked up by 6:45 P.M. *Astoria* took in a handful of York-towners, and Buckmaster transferred to the cruiser at 5:44 P.M. *Benham* rescued 721; *Balch*, 545; *Russell*, 492; *Anderson*, 203; *Morris*, 246; *Hammann*, 85; and *Hughes*, 24. All together, more than 2,300 Yorktowners were saved.

Chapter Fifteen

★ ★ ★ ★ ★ ★ ★

★ ★ ★ Even as *Yorktown* was being torpedoed by planes from *Hiryu*, her dive bombers were seeking out the enemy. At 2:30 P.M., Lieutenant Sam Adams—his squadron mates called him the blond Viking—spotted the last remaining Japanese carrier. He circled in and out of the clouds, taking his time, checking and double-checking his position. At 2:45 P.M. he communicated his discovery by radiotelephone in plain English. As a double check, his radioman sent out the same information by telegraphic key.

Enterprise picked up the message. "Have sighted one enemy carrier," it read, "one battleship, two heavy cruisers, and four destroyers. Position is thirty-one degrees, fifteen minutes north; one hundred seventy-five degrees, five minutes west. Steaming due north at fifteen knots."

Adams' report was nearly perfect. He had pinned down *Hiryu*'s location precisely, and the battleship he had seen was *Haruna*.* The heavy cruisers were *Tone* and *Chikuma*. There were only three destroyers, *Kazagumo*, *Yugumo*, and *Makigumo*. The fourth destroyer reported by Adams

---

* *Haruna* was supposedly sunk at the outset of the war by American hero Colin Kelly. However, she led a charmed life; many claimed that they had sunk her; no one ever did. She finished her war, decks awash, but superstructure above water, at the Japanese naval base at Kure.

was, in fact, *Nagara*, a light cruiser that looked very much like the big destroyers.

At 2:50 P.M. *Enterprise* put up her strike—ten of her own dive bombers commanded by Lieutenant Wilmer Gallaher and fourteen of *Yorktown*'s refugees led by Lieutenant Dave Shumway, senior officer in Bombing 3 now that Leslie and Holmberg were out of it. Gallaher, as leader of both groups, ordered *Yorktown*'s planes to stand off when they sighted the fourth Japanese carrier, while he and five *Enterprise* shipmates went for it. The idea was that once Gallaher's planes had taken care of *Hiryu*, Shumway and his *Yorktown* planes could go after the battleship and the cruisers.

Both sides were by now close to exhaustion. *Hiryu*'s log shows that so far that day her Zeros and gunners had battled nearly six dozen American aircraft. Now here were two dozen more. The Americans were just as tired. Ensign Sid Bottomley of *Yorktown* had started the day with a scanty breakfast and an early-morning search flight. He had come back to *Yorktown*, snatched a single cup of coffee while his Dauntless was being refueled, and joined Lieutenant Commander Max Leslie in the attack on the carrier *Kaga*; he had scored one hit. He had escaped through a hail of gunfire and a swarm of Zeros only to find on returning that his own ship was under attack. He had orbited near *Yorktown* until he had nearly run out of gas, then had landed on *Enterprise*.

Bottomley had been awake for eleven hours and in the air most of that time. Before he took off against *Hiryu*, he went to *Enterprise*'s ready room, his throat parched and his stomach groaning. Someone handed him a sandwich, and he bolted down three or four immense bites before he realized that he was eating, of all things, peanut butter. So, here he was, over a Japanese carrier again, hungry, thirsty, and tired, bits of peanut butter sticking to his teeth.

Six *Enterprise* planes, led by Gallaher, came out of the clouds and almost caught *Hiryu* by surprise. The carrier's captain, however, was agile; he spun *Hiryu* hard right, and at thirty knots, she swiftly shifted course from north to southeast. Gallaher and his men, outmaneuvered, missed their target. *Yorktown's* Shumway, suspecting that this might happen, led his planes around so that they could attack *Hiryu* from the southwest, out of the sun. This pilot had no intention of being left to attack the battleship or the cruisers; he wanted *Hiryu*, the carrier that had struck *Yorktown*.

Eleven of Shumway's planes carried 1,000-pound bombs; the other three, along with the *Enterprise* planes, carried 500-pounders. All of Shumway's planes began their attack, with at least a dozen Zeros trying to cut them down, for *Hiryu* was, after all, the only landing field they had to return to within thousands of miles.

Lieutenant (jg) Gordon Sherwood began his dive at 18,000 feet. "Fighters in echelon," he recalled later, "made sweeping scissors back and forth across my tail." The Zeros used their 7.7-millimeter guns to mark the range and only then began firing with their heavier 20-millimeter cannon. Sherwood also remarked the skill with which they flew. "At the top of my dive a Zero fighter pulled up from the tail of the preceding plane and dove at me."

The Zeros did the best they could. Shumway's plane was evidence enough of that; the diving and landing flaps, the stabilizer, elevator, right main gas tank, rudder, fuselage, and engine all were hit. His gunner, Ray Coons, was shot in the arm. Randy Cooner's dive bomber was peppered by 7.7 fire, and two 20-millimeter shells damaged his radio equipment, shredded his life raft, and wounded his gunner, C. R. Bassett, who kept right on firing, bringing down a Zero and driving off a float plane. Bud Merrill's plane was hit from underneath, and his gunner, D. J. Bergeron, was wounded; shrapnel from a cannon burst cut his feet.

Ensign John Butler and Lieutenant (jg) Obie Wiseman were shot down. Their gunners, D. D. Berg and G. V. Dawn, died with them.

In spite of the fierce opposition, Shumway and his York-towners scored hits on *Hiryu*. Four 1,000-pound bombs burst on the forward part of the carrier's flight deck, just ahead of the portside bridge structure, and she was left "burning furiously," Shumway reported later. He and the other pilots hightailed it to the northeast, rendezvousing in groups for mutual protection against enraged Zero pilots.

Two of Shumway's pilots, Ensigns Bob Campbell and Bob Benson, went for the battleship and one of the cruisers once they had seen how badly the carrier had been hurt. Several hits were claimed, but in fact they both had scored only near-misses. Toward the end of the attack three pilots from *Yorktown's* other squadron—they had been scouting when they heard Adams' radio report of the Japanese position—showed up to lend a hand. They were Ensign Ben Preston, Lieutenant Wally Short, and Lieutenant (jg) John Neilsen. Preston stated later that he was almost certain that he had struck *Hiryu* and that Short and Neilsen had scored near-misses.

Fires broke out on *Hiryu's* hangar and flight decks. Below, her engineers battled furiously to save the ship, but it was hopeless. In a few hours *Hiryu* stopped dead in the water and listed heavily. Captain Tomeo Kaku ordered her abandoned; he and Rear Admiral Tamon Yamaguchi, heartbroken, elected to go down with the ship. The two lashed themselves to the helm and waited for her to sink. But *Hiryu* was almost as stubborn about sinking as *Yorktown* had been; hours went by, and she was still afloat. Impatient at this state of affairs, the two officers went below and committed suicide. It was not until 5:10 A.M. the next morning that *Hiryu* finally went down. Even then she had to be given a hand as she was scuttled.* *Yorktown,* half-crippled when she had left Pearl Harbor, could chalk up her third enemy carrier.

Shumway and the eleven other surviving *Yorktown* planes made it safely back to *Enterprise,* although Shumway's, Cooner's, and Merrill's planes were so badly shot up that they would never fly again. The pilots were exhilarated, for although their own ship was smoking and abandoned, they had extracted a telling measure of revenge.

The Japanese situation by now was desperate indeed, but Yamamoto was not yet prepared to concede the battle. Enemy hopes were higher than they should have been because Admiral Nagumo, as darkness fell, was misled into thinking that *two* American carriers had been destroyed. Earlier in the day his pilots had reported that an American carrier was "burning fiercely." Nagumo wrote

---

* *Soryu* sank at 7:13 P.M. on June 4. *Kaga* sank twelve minutes later. *Akagi,* like *Hiryu,* had to be scuttled, going down at 5 A.M. on June 5, just ten minutes ahead of *Hiryu.* By dawn on the morning of June 5 all four carriers in the enemy's main striking force were at the bottom of the Pacific. *Yorktown,* although abandoned, was still afloat.

off the carrier; it was *Yorktown*. Now, at the end of the day, a float plane from *Chikuma* reported sighting an American carrier of the *Yorktown* class, adrift. Nagumo concluded that this was a second carrier, when actually it was again *Yorktown*.

Nagumo's hopes were crushed not much later when the same pilot from *Chikuma* spotted *Enterprise* and *Hornet* and reported his finding at once. The pilot, taking cover in cloud formations when necessary in evading American fighters, found the two American carriers a second time. But somehow he must have lost his bearings—everyone by this point was weary and confused. Whatever the reason, he reported his second finding as two *more* carriers.

Nagumo, whose heart had never been entirely in this battle to begin with, was now totally confused. He was very certain that his pilots had knocked out two carriers. Yet here was a scout pilot reporting four more carriers, all of them operational. That would mean the Americans had opened the battle with six carriers, and Japanese intelligence had never indicated that the Americans could put together that kind of force.

Shortly before 11 P.M., Nagumo sent a message to Yamamoto: "There are still four enemy aircraft carriers, possibly including light aircraft carriers, six cruisers, and sixteen destroyers. They are steaming westward. None of our aircraft carriers is operational. We plan to contact the enemy with scout aircraft tomorrow morning."

Tomorrow morning? That would never do, for hours earlier *Yamamoto* had radioed Tokyo that the American fleet was nearly destroyed and that what was left of it was retreating eastward. It was more a hopeful prophecy than a statement of fact. To make it foolproof, Yamamoto had ordered his two carriers in the Aleutians, *Ryujo* and *Junyo*, to join him; they were on the way. The carrier *Zuiho*, with the troop convoy, was moving up from the southwest. And within sight of the flagship *Yamato* was the ancient *Hosho*, the world's first carrier built from the keel up. Perhaps, Yamamoto thought, he was inferior to the Americans in aircraft strength, even with these reinforcements, but he still had overwhelming superiority in total number of ships and guns.

What Yamamoto had wanted all along—and what he wanted now—was a decisive fleet engagement. Nagumo's state of mind, he had decided, was hardly conducive to a slashing night attack. Thus, Yamamoto fired off a message, relieving Nagumo of the command of the main carrier force and its escorting ships. Vice Admiral Nobutake Kondo, commander of the invasion force, was ordered to take over. Kondo, at the time, was steaming full speed with his heavy surface warships to join Nagumo.

Yamamoto wanted first to destroy Midway, to eliminate it as an aircraft base. To do this, he sent out orders at 8:30 P.M. to Lieutenant Commander Yahachi Tanabe and his submarine, *I-168*, still patrolling off Midway, to close in on the island and, with its four-inch deck gun, to begin shelling the airfield. It was to maintain its attack until joined by the four heavy cruisers from Kondo's invasion group— *Mikuma, Mogami, Suzuya,* and *Kumano,* then the most powerful ships of their class in the world.

At 1 A.M. on June 5, Commander Tanabe poked his

---

* They were the famous cheat cruisers, supposedly built with six-inch guns and tonnage within limits imposed by the Washington Naval Disarmament Treaty (1922). In 1938 these ships had been secretly refitted with the eight-inch guns for which they had been designed. Carrying a total of forty of these big rifles, they could have given Midway a very bad time of it.

periscope above the ocean's surface just off Midway. He was anxious to get into the fight, for since the war had begun he had taken part in no real combat. In the months just before and after Pearl Harbor, he had been the skipper of the second-line submarine RO-59, training officers and men within the placid confines of the Japanese Inland Sea. He had taken command of I-168 in January, 1942, after Lieutenant Commander Otoji Nakamura had brought her home from sentry duty off the island of Oahu in Hawaii.

At 1:30 A.M., Tanabe surfaced, and the first deck gun round winged toward Midway. Five more followed in quick succession before two searchlights on shore pinpointed the submarine. Shore batteries began firing back, and their aim was very effective. Shells bracketed I-168 almost at once; a disappointed Tanabe had no choice but to "pull the plug" and beat a hasty retreat. He headed south, away from the island, shaking off surface pursuers. Angry and disappointed, Tanabe assumed that I-168 had finished its job for this battle.

At this point Yamamoto was almost prepared to admit defeat. He might question Nagumo's will to fight; but he knew that he could not escape Nagumo's professional judgment, and that judgment indicated to Nagumo, and now to Yamamoto, that the enemy still had four aircraft carriers. If Yamamoto pushed east to engage the enemy ships, he might not find them until dawn, and again those deadly dive bombers would be upon him. At 2:55 A.M., Yamamoto reached the most difficult decision of his long and celebrated career: "Occupation of Midway is canceled," he signaled his fleet. The four heavy cruisers that were steaming to join the submarine I-168 off Midway turned back, and the entire remainder of the Japanese fleet began to withdraw from the area. Yamamoto, who had been a shrewd, aggressive cardplayer when he had been stationed in Washington in the 1920's, was folding his hand: he ordered all his ships to rendezvous with rear-echelon tankers to take on the fuel they would need for the long, sad voyage home.

Admiral Spruance, to whom Admiral Fletcher had by now largely given over command (Spruance retained in his task force the only two operational carriers), was not aware of these developments, but he did sense the danger of a night action. The Japanese were trained intensively in night combat, and Yamamoto had eleven battleships with him. Against them, at night, American aircraft, without radar and without special training, were almost entirely useless.

Thus, the American ships withdrew to the east, in order to avoid a showdown with superior Japanese guns in a night action. Spruance was prepared to turn west again at dawn, and then—and only then—to look for the enemy.

The ships standing by *Yorktown* began moving to the east at 6 P.M. on June 4, leaving the carrier alone, except for the destroyer *Hughes*, which had orders to sink her if she began to burn, for fire would give her position away and make possible her capture by the Japanese.

There is no question that Spruance acted properly in withdrawing to the east. There has ever since been some sharp challenging of the decision to leave *Yorktown* with only a single destroyer for defense. She was still afloat and, to some, seemed to be listing at a less dangerous angle. Fletcher and Buckmaster, some critics still contend, should have put a salvage party aboard her on the night of June 4. This is, of course, another after-the-fact judgment. One thing can be said: early in the evening of June 4, Buckmaster was making plans to salvage his ship. Perhaps even more to the point, the Navy in those days had no standard operation for salvage parties. *Yorktown* did not have a group specifically organized for such an activity. And her crew, it must be remembered, were scattered, most of them exhausted and shoeless, among eight different ships.

Buckmaster, aboard the cruiser *Astoria*, never gave up the idea that *Yorktown* might still be saved. He and the officers most intimately concerned with salvage operations stayed up most of the night of June 4 and 5 studying methods for doing the job. Lieutenant Hurlbert changed ships twelve times that night, searching out key men to make up a salvage party; all of them were gathered into a group aboard *Astoria*.

First, it was decided, the flight decks and hangar decks would have to be cleared of debris, including aircraft, to lighten ship. Next, gunner's mates and shipfitters would cut loose and cast away the four five-inch guns on the port side. With power furnished by escorting ships, water and oil could be pumped from *Yorktown*'s port tanks to the starboard. This, it was reasoned, would bring *Yorktown* back to an almost even keel. Finally, water tenders would light off the boilers, and *Yorktown* could limp to port under her own power. All this might be hastened because the fleet tug *Vireo*, moored at French Frigate Shoal, between Midway and Oahu, was already on her way to take *Yorktown* in tow while the work progressed.

What *Yorktown* needed was a great deal of hard work

and a little bit of luck. At 6:26 A.M. on June 5, the destroyer *Hughes*, maintaining her lonely patrol around *Yorktown*, picked up a Japanese scout plane on her radar. It was another float plane from the cruiser *Chikuma*. The pilot, at 6:52 A.M., radioed to his forces: "I see an enemy aircraft carrier of the *Yorktown* class. It is listing to starboard [*sic*] and drifting. Position is one hundred and eleven degrees true bearing, distance two hundred and forty miles from my takeoff point. One destroyer is nearby."

The Japanese immediately radioed Submarine *I-168* and Commander Tanabe: "*I-168* will locate and destroy the American carrier." *Yorktown*'s position was given as 150 miles northeast of Midway. "We set off at once," Tanabe reported after the war. "My electrical officer, Lieutenant Mochizuki, gave amulets to each member of the crew." Mochizuki, a religious man, had obtained the good luck charms at Suitengu Shrine, a temple in Fukuoka on the southern Japanese island of Kyushu. Each of the 104 members of the crew was wearing one of them as Tanabe circled Midway and set course for *Yorktown*'s estimated position.

Aboard the destroyer *Hughes*, at almost the same time that *I-168* was clearing Midway, machine gun fire was heard, and men on deck noticed splashes in the water near them. They followed the line made by the splashes until they saw a man in *Yorktown*'s port catwalk, firing one of her machine guns. A whaleboat crew from *Hughes* promptly boarded the carrier and picked up Seaman Norman Pichette, who had been wounded in the stomach by shrapnel and had somehow been overlooked when *Yorktown* had been abandoned. The original wound had not been serious, but peritonitis had set in, and Pichette died, less than twenty-four hours after he whispered to his rescuers that there was still another man aboard *Yorktown*.

The whaleboat returned to *Yorktown* and picked up Seaman George Weise, unconscious and suffering from a skull fracture and other injuries. Both he and Pichette had been in the carrier's sick bay and had probably been overlooked in the darkness or had been presumed dead. Weise, who recovered, regained consciousness in *Hughes'* sick bay as a doctor was giving him blood. Minutes later Ensign Harry Gibbs came paddling up to *Hughes* in a rubber life raft. He and his Wildcat had been shot down the day before, and he had been trying to get to *Yorktown* all night. "I must have rowed six or seven miles," Gibbs estimated.

A short time later the fleet tug *Vireo*, from French Frigate Shoal, came over the horizon and began to make preparations to take *Yorktown* in tow. Sailors from *Hughes*, after making a third trip to *Yorktown*, reported that the carrier seemed to be holding her own. The fire in the rag room had flared up again, but that did not seem to pose serious danger.

Almost simultaneously, miles to the east, Captain Buckmaster, 28 of his officers, and 133 enlisted men had transferred aboard the destroyer *Hammann* and started west to reboard the carrier.

Chapter Sixteen

★ ★ ★ ★ ★ ★ ★

★ ★ ★ The destroyer *Hammann*, carrying Captain Buckmaster and 161 members of his crew, pulled alongside *Yorktown* at 4:40 A.M. (Midway time) on June 6, almost thirty-eight hours from the time that the abandon-ship order had been given. By then nearly all the other York-towners were on their way to Pearl Harbor aboard the submarine tender *Fulton*, which had been sent out specifically to fetch them home. Also alongside *Yorktown*, by dawn on June 6, were the destroyers *Hughes*, *Monaghan*, *Gwin*, *Balch*, and *Benham*. The fleet tug *Vireo* had put a line over *Yorktown*'s bow, but with the carrier's rudder jammed to port, towing her was slow and tedious. The best speed *Vireo* could make was three knots.*

Frank Boo, a yeoman on Admiral Fletcher's staff and a member of the salvage party, later reported, "I convinced the admiral that I should go back and recover the important Coral Sea battle report. It was like going aboard a ghost ship. Everything was so still. The only sound I heard

---

* *Yorktown*'s planes were still in action, which had now turned into pursuit of the enemy. Members of Wally Short's Scouting 5 accompanied *Hornet* planes on a strike in midafternoon on June 5. They missed the main enemy fleet, but all joined in attacking a lone destroyer, *Tanikaze*, which they came across on the way back to *Hornet*. During the engagement Lieutenant Sam Adams was shot down and killed.

227

was the lapping of water against her deck. It was dark everywhere belowdecks, and the upper decks were slippery from oil and water. It was impossible to walk without a handhold on something. All kinds of stuff was adrift— life jackets, shoes, torpedoes, airplanes, the personal gear of the men who had abandoned two days before."

Lieutenant Commander Aldrich and his assistant, Oxy Hurlbert (transferred from gunnery to damage control just prior to the Battle of Midway), made a quick appraisal of *Yorktown's* condition and reported their findings to Buckmaster.

The only damage of consequence from the first bomb attack was confined to the rag stowage locker forward, where the fire was still burning. Aldrich and Hurlbert were able to report to Buckmaster that they thought it probably could be put out easily. The most serious damage was a consequence of the torpedo hits from the second attack. All three firerooms on the port side, including a superheater fireroom, were flooded. The generator room just forward of them was also flooded. Berthing compartments and two mess halls immediately above the firerooms were demolished and flooded to a height of eight feet. A number of quick-closing watertight doors, weakened by the bombs taken during Coral Sea, had been sprung, so that water was leaking into the two main engine rooms. *Yorktown* was open to the sea for almost one-sixth of her length on the port side, but with the watertight doors leaking, she was taking water into compartments that made up one-third of her length. Nothing could be done, it was decided, until the ship's list, now estimated at about twenty-seven degrees, was corrected.

Gunner's mates and shipfitters, under Gunner Maurice Witting, started cutting away the first (most forward) of the four five-inch guns on Yorktown's port side. Another detail began jettisoning debris over the side, and engineers worked out a plan to shift fuel supplies from the port side to starboard.

Hammann, the most powerful of the escorting destroyers, pulled alongside and moored to Yorktown's starboard side, which was jutting high out of the water. Two hoses charged with foamite were pulled aboard the carrier and worked forward for fighting fires. As a precaution, another was attached to the flight deck fire-fighting system. A fourth was connected to Yorktown's empty starboard fuel tanks; through this hose, Hammann pumped her own bilge into the carrier.

Chief Joe Kisela, with four of his best shipfitters—Vance Brazile, Paul Vander, Norris Hook, and Clyde Upchurch —went forward to battle the fire in the stowage locker, and with surprising ease, it was eventually extinguished.

With a pump from Hammann, water was sucked from the after engine room. On the hangar deck, detonators were removed from torpedoes, and damaged planes stowed overhead on the port side were given the "deep six."

Yeoman Boo recovered the Coral Sea battle report, and Commander Ralph Arnold, the supply officer, recovered the crew's pay records.

At about 1 P.M. Midway time, Yorktown's salvage crew knocked off for lunch.* Most of the crew gathered on the

---

* Yorktown's pilots had already put in a good day's work, seventeen of her dive bombers having taken part in an attack on two of the Japanese cheat cruisers, Mogami and Mikuma, which had earlier collided in their attempts to pull away from the American submarine Tambor. Six hits were made on the

hangar deck for sandwiches, warm Coca-Cola, and tomato juice. The destroyer *Balch* stood in to send over a whale-boat to the carrier with a message, and as soon as the whale-boat returned, *Balch* resumed her place in the defending screen of destroyers, steaming counterclockwise around *Yorktown* and *Hammann*, one mile distant. Each of the five destroyers carried sonar equipment, and the sonar set of each was working, listening for submarines.

Shipfitter Earl Fogarty, one of several members of the salvage crew eating lunch on the starboard side of *York-town's* hangar deck, near the Number 1 elevator, later re-called that Chief Joe Kisela, glancing out to sea past *Ham-mann*, said, "Hey, look! There's some blackfish," and that Shipfitter Clyde Upchurch, looking where Kisela was pointing, shouted, "Blackfish, hell. Those are torpedoes."

Torpedoes they were, from Commander Tanabe's *I-168*, which had penetrated the destroyer screen and fired from what was almost point-blank range. It was one of the great submarine exploits of the war, and Tanabe has described how he did it in his own words:*

> We set off at once [after receiving orders to sink *York-town*], running submerged in daylight hours at the best speed we could make and still nurse our batteries. After dark I ran on the surface, but could not use top speed for fear of missing our target in the blackness. So it was that at 5:30 A.M., on June 6 . . . my best-trained lookout

two ships, one of them by Ensign Ben Preston of *Yorktown*. *Mikuma* was sunk, and although *Mogami* got away, she was so badly damaged that after reaching Japan, she did not put to sea again for two years.

* He told his story after the war to Joseph D. Harrington, co-author of this book, in Japan, where Harrington was stationed as a chief journalist in the Navy. Tanabe's first-person story, related with Mr. Harrington's assistance, first appeared in the *United States Naval Institute Proceedings*.

picked up *Yorktown*. She was a black shape on the horizon, about 11 miles distant. It was the easiest intercept a submarine commander ever made. My course had not changed, from beginning to end.

Yorktown was approximately eleven miles distant and slightly to the right of *I-168's* course, when first sighted. Tanabe submerged, changed course to the northeast, reduced speed to six knots, and leveled his submarine off at a depth of ninety feet. As he closed in, he further reduced speed until it was below three knots. Periodically he took the boat up to a depth of sixty feet, from which point its periscope could be raised above the surface. It required only a few small adjustments in course to keep *I-168's* bow and her torpedo tubes headed straight for *Yorktown's* starboard beam. Tanabe explained:

> Our screws were barely turning over as we drew closer, and I hoped they were not giving off enough turbulence for the American ships to detect us on their sound equipment. I had sighted one destroyer ahead of the carrier with a towline out to her [actually the fleet tug *Vireo*] and another destroyer nestled close to *Yorktown's* side. Three more kept station on the side I was approaching, which made me feel certain there must be at least two more on the opposite side. This meant seven of them against one of us.
>
> Each time I took a sight, the sun was higher in the sky. *Yorktown* appeared to be making just a little headway. I kept making minor changes of course to keep *I-168* headed at her midship section. I knew that we might get sunk in this action, but before that happened, I meant to do the maximum possible damage to this ship. I wanted my torpedoes to plow into her midsection, not her bow or stern.

All *I-168* men limited their movements to the most necessary ones only, fearing to create some sound the American detectors might pick up. By 11 A.M., I had decided that the enemy equipment was not very sensitive. This gave me confidence as the range shortened; I kept moving in.

Suddenly my sound operator reported that the Americans had stopped emitting detection signals. I couldn't understand this but, since it was nearly noon, I tried to make my voice light and told my crew, "It appears the Americans have interrupted their war for lunch. Now is our chance to strike them good and hard while they are eating!" There were small jokes made about what to give them for dessert. Shortly thereafter I raised the periscope again.

Abaft my beam, each about 1,000 yards distant, were a pair of American destroyers, one to port, one to starboard. *I-168* had safely pierced the protective screen of escorts; I could now give the order to fire.

Then I took another look. *Yorktown* and her hugging destroyer filled my periscope lens. I was too close! At that moment I estimated my range at 600 yards or less. It was necessary to come around again and open up the range. What I had to do now was to try to escape detection by those destroyers above us and get far enough away so that my torpedoes, fired from a 60-foot depth, would have enough running space to stabilize themselves at a 19-foot depth for hitting.*

I kept *I-168* in a right hand circle, easing the rudder a little so that I could return to my original track at a point about one mile from *Yorktown*. I didn't dare put up the periscope until the compass showed us back on our original

---

* Tanabe was never picked up by American detection equipment during his approach. Oil leaking from *Yorktown* could have affected conditions, or there may have existed a thermal gradient, a layer of warm water below the surface that will deflect sound beams upward before they strike a target and are reflected back again.

course. So I concentrated instead on a torpedo tactic I wanted to use. Though some submarines in 1942 had Model 95 torpedoes—underwater versions of the very powerful Model 93 "Long Lance" used on surface ships—my torpedoes were an older type. Model 95s had 991-pound warheads; mine had 446-pound ones. So I planned to make two torpedoes into one. If I followed usual procedure and fired my four torpedoes all at once, with a two-degree spread, they would cover six degrees. But I wanted very badly to deprive the Americans of this carrier. I intended to limit my salvo to a two-degree spread. I would fire No. 1 and No. 2 first, two degrees apart, then send No. 3 and No. 4 in their wakes, on the same courses. This way, I could achieve two large hits instead of four small ones. I could thus deliver all my punch into the carrier's midsection rather than spread it out along her hull.

When I was back on my approach course, I took another look, and shook my head at how the destroyers still seemed unaware of us. Either they were poor sailors, had poor equipment, or *I-168* was a charmed vessel. At a range of 1,200 yards, my periscope up, I sent my four torpedoes away as planned. I did not lower the periscope then, either. The wakes of my torpedoes could be seen, so their source could be quickly established. And, if *I-168* was going to die, I at least wanted the satisfaction of seeing whether our fish hit home.

Less than a minute later we heard the explosions. *"Banzai!"* someone shouted. "Go ahead at full speed!" I ordered, and then, "Take her down to 200 feet!"

As Tanabe had guessed, the wakes from his torpedoes were spotted by the Americans, first by the men having lunch on *Yorktown*'s hangar deck, then by sailors aboard the destroyer *Hammann*. One of *Hammann*'s sailors ran to a twenty-millimeter gun and opened fire at the torpedoes, hoping that the slugs would detonate their warheads. The gunfire was heard on board both ships, and frantic warnings were sounded.

Lieutenant Hurlbert, on *Yorktown's* bridge when *Hammann's* gun began firing, ran down to the hangar deck, joining Buckmaster. He later clearly remembered seeing the torpedoes heading for *Yorktown*. Somehow they reminded him of the view from the foot of San Francisco's Market Street. The wakes, he said, looked like "two pairs of streetcar tracks."

Lieutenant Cundiff was outboard of the hangar deck, in a boat pocket, when the torpedoes were first spotted. With him was William "Pinky" Davis, a water tender. Davis, seeing that *Hammann* was casting off her mooring lines to get out of the line of fire, swung down to the destroyer's deck. Cundiff, making a more careful assessment of the situation, decided that *Hammann* had no chance to get clear, and he leaped through a porthole into *Yorktown's* photographic laboratory. Moments later Davis was thrown into the sea and suffered fatal injuries when *Hammann's* depth charges went off.

One of the four torpedoes fired by *I-168* ran wild, passing ahead of *Yorktown* and astern of the destroyer *Balch*. Another ran shallow, catching *Hammann* amidships and exploding in her Number 2 fireroom. Tanabe's two remaining torpedoes passed under *Hammann* and struck *Yorktown* in her unarmored belly, exposed by the heavy list to port, where, at 1:34 P.M., they exploded almost exactly opposite the point at which the two aircraft torpedoes had penetrated two days earlier.

Hammann, her back broken, sank within two minutes.

At 1:38, *Yorktown* was rocked again by two more intense explosions, one occurring as seawater reached the sinking *Hammann*'s hot boilers, the other from the destroyer's own depth charges.*

The two explosions from *Hammann* rocked *Yorktown* almost as forcefully as the two *I-168* torpedoes. Lieutenant Commander Davis, thrown from a *Yorktown* catwalk into the ocean when the torpedoes went off, had his back broken when *Hammann* exploded. The effect of the *Hammann* underwater explosions on the men thrown into the ocean by the preceding torpedo blasts was devastating. *Yorktown*'s Meade Murphy reported, "I saw bodies come to the surface afterward. Some had their insides blown out through their mouths. Some had no arms."

Of *Hammann*'s 251-man ship's company, 81 were dead or missing, and another 85 were injured. Of the injured, 26 died after being taken out of the sea. Only one-third of her crew escaped death or injury. Commander True suffered two broken ribs when he was smashed against a chart ta-

* Commander Arnold True, *Hammann*'s skipper, believes that the depth charges may have been set off by one of the destroyer's own torpedoes, which could have been driven free of its tube with the steering apparatus damaged when *Hammann* was hit. The torpedo then could have made a circular run, returning to strike *Hammann* and starting a chain detonation among the destroyer's depth charges. The explanation is somewhat questionable. When *Hammann* first went alongside *Yorktown* on June 6, her depth charges were reported to Commander True as having been set on "safe," meaning that they would not go off even if they were cast overboard. When the torpedo wakes from *I-168* were sighted, *Hammann* began casting loose in order to pursue the enemy submarine. This means that two explanations are possible: either the earlier report to True on the "safe" setting of depth charges was erroneous, or as *Hammann* was being cast off from *Yorktown*, a crew member began readying the depth charges for attacking *I-168*, thus putting them in a condition other than "safe" at the moment *Hammann* sank. Chief Bob Powell, of *Yorktown*, reported seeing on *Hammann*'s stern someone (later identified as Torpedoman Berlyn Kimbrel, awarded the Navy Cross) who was both helping other destroyermen get off their ship and working on the depth charges at the time *Hammann* disappeared from sight.

ble and thrown overboard. When he recovered from the shock, he discovered that he was holding two men's heads above water; both of them were dead.

The destroyers *Gwin, Monaghan,* and *Hughes* immediately formed a scouting line and began to search for *I-168.** The destroyer *Balch* continued to patrol around *Yorktown,* while *Benham* and the fleet tug *Vireo* moved in to recover survivors.

The Japanese torpedoes that gutted *Yorktown* could not have been more perfectly placed. Six of the carrier's nine boiler rooms, plus both her engine rooms, were now flooded, and she began settling in the water. "The only good thing about it," said Signalman Charles Thomas, "was that the list was lessened to about seventeen degrees, and we could walk around the decks a little better."

Still aboard *Yorktown,* Buckmaster called for volunteers to spend the night aboard the carrier, expecting that the destroyers—once they had sunk the Japanese submarine

---

* Tanabe estimates that the American destroyers dropped sixty depth charges in an effort to sink him; his count is probably high, but the attack was indeed spirited. "The sixtieth depth charge," Tanabe reported, "landed just off my bow. It put out all the lights, causing small leaks in many places, and this made chlorine gas form in my forward battery room." The deadly gas is a submariner's greatest fear. Tanabe watched as a mouse "staggered drunkenly across my foot." Then, unexpectedly, the American destroyers broke off the attack. They had been ordered back to *Yorktown* to investigate sound contacts picked up by *Balch* and *Benham.* Tanabe, puzzled but relieved, took *I-168* to the surface, thus using up most of his remaining compressed air. "When I got to the bridge, there was no sign of the enemy carrier. But between myself and the eastern horizon I could see three American destroyers." One of them, *Hughes,* saw *I-168* surface. All three destroyers—*Hughes, Gwin,* and *Monaghan* —came about and started pursuit. Tanabe, taking advantage of every second, continued to charge his batteries and refill his air tanks, even as *Hughes* came within range and opened up with her forward five-inch gun. At the last moment Tanabe submerged, turned 180 degrees, and ran directly under the American destroyers. The trick worked, and *I-168* escaped. Tanabe arrived at Kure, his home port, with one ton of fuel oil remaining. He and *I-168* were hailed as heroes, and Midway was celebrated as a great Japanese victory. One of Japan's great sailors, he later commanded another submarine, *I-176,* managed a number of daredevil escapes, and survived the war.

—would be able to return to her side to supply the power needed to continue to right her. But conditions were now far too dangerous, Buckmaster's officers advised him. For the second time, Buckmaster reluctantly ordered *Yorktown* abandoned. The captain, in keeping with ancient naval tradition, waited until he thought he was the last to leave his ship before he lowered himself into a rescue boat. Unknown to Buckmaster, Lieutenant Commander Delaney and Machinist P. N. MacDonald had remained aboard to close any watertight doors they found open.

When Buckmaster saw Delaney and MacDonald appear on *Yorktown*'s fantail, he attempted to climb back up the line to his ship, but he was too exhausted to make it. He and the other Yorktowners spent the rest of the night in the patrolling destroyers, waiting for dawn and another chance to save their carrier.

Hurlbert spent the night in the wardroom of the destroyer *Gwin*, when one of her officers nudged him awake the next morning as the sun edged over the horizon. "You'd better get topside if you want to get a last look at your big silver baby," the officer said to Hurlbert. "She's about to go over."

A great ship, when she goes down, is supposed to be a noble sight. *Yorktown*'s death was noisy and ugly. She lay on the Pacific exhausted, her back broken by four torpedoes and one of *Hammann*'s depth charges. She turned over slowly and sank, airplanes and heavy equipment rattling and grinding around inside her, four years, eight months, and seven days after she had been commissioned.

Epilogue

★ ★ ★ ★ ★ ★ ★

★ ★ ★ The destroyers *Gwin* and *Benham* combed the debris for survivors and then turned for Pearl Harbor, carrying the living from *Yorktown* and *Hammann.* The other three destroyers rejoined *Enterprise* and *Hornet,* and *Vireo* set course for Midway.

The decisive battle for the Pacific was over. Yamamoto, defeated and frustrated, began his ultimate retreat at 5 A.M. on June 7, at precisely the hour *Yorktown* sank.

Captain Buckmaster wrote his loss-of-ship report with mingled sorrow and pride. "I have nothing but praise for the fighting, aggressive spirit of the *Yorktown* personnel," he said. Then he listed the engagements the ship had taken a part in:

> Marshall and Gilbert islands—Jan. 31 ,1942.
> Salamaua and Lae—March 10, 1942.
> Tulagi (3 attacks)—May 4, 1942.
> Sinking of enemy CV, Misima Island—May 7, 1942.
> Night action with enemy carrier planes—May 7, 1942.
> Battle of Coral Sea—May 8, 1942.
> Battle of Midway—June 4-7, 1942.

The engagements in the Gilberts, at Salamaua and Lae (the attack over the Owen Stanley Mountains), and at Tulagi had been a good bit less than impressive. But *Yorktown* had learned from her mistakes. That learning had paid off, as Captain Buckmaster indicated, in the "sinking of enemy CV" on May 7. What he was referring to was the sinking of the Japanese carrier *Shoho*; planes from both *Lexington* and *Yorktown* had attacked *Shoho. Yorktown* planes had scored with twelve bombs and four torpedoes and surely deserved at least 80 percent of the credit for the kill. The following day *Yorktown*'s planes had dropped two bombs on the big Japanese carrier *Shokaku*; one of them fell from Jo-Jo Powers' cripped dive bomber. *Shokaku* was badly damaged and was forced to put back to the Inland Sea for repairs. That same day *Yorktown* was badly damaged by a Japanese bomb that exploded in an aviation storeroom, directly above the main engine room.

Yorktown had returned to sea after temporary repairs and, on June 4, dropped four bombs on the Japanese carrier *Kaga*. Later that same day she was hit by three bombs and two aircraft torpedoes and abandoned. Even after she had been abandoned, her pilots and planes, flying from *Enterprise*, dropped four bombs on the Japanese carrier *Hiryu*. On June 6, *Yorktown* was finished off by two torpedoes from *I-168*.

By ordnance statistics, *Yorktown* gave more than she took. She scored with twenty-two bomb hits on four enemy carriers, sank *Kaga* and *Hiryu* without help, and sank *Shoho* with only a little help. She helped chew up *Zuikaku*'s air complement so badly that the ship could not fight at Midway, and she put *Shokaku* out of action without assistance, all within a period of twenty-three days. In the same time span she was hit by four bombs and four torpedoes.

Never before had one American warship suffered so much and dealt out so much punishment to others.

In writing his report, Buckmaster had this to say:

> It is our sincerest wish to man another carrier as soon as possible. It is strongly urged that an organization which has worked together under war conditions for more than a year should be kept together if possible. Results count— and it is recommended that a crew which has already produced such results be given the opportunity to keep counting.

Buckmaster himself never held another command at sea; perhaps that was only coincidental, or perhaps it was a reflection on the loss of *Yorktown*. He later held shore commands at Norfolk, Kansas City, and San Diego, moved on to become Commander, Western Carolines and Southern Area, and finished out the war as Commander, South China Naval Forces. He retired as a vice admiral in November, 1946, and twenty years later was living in peaceful Coronado, California. On a sunny afternoon a visitor might find him there on the golf course, relaxing with one or more of his former *Yorktown* shipmates and reminiscing about a certain aircraft carrier and the part she played in the battles of the Coral Sea and Midway.

INDEX

Index

★ ★ ★ ★ ★ ★ ★

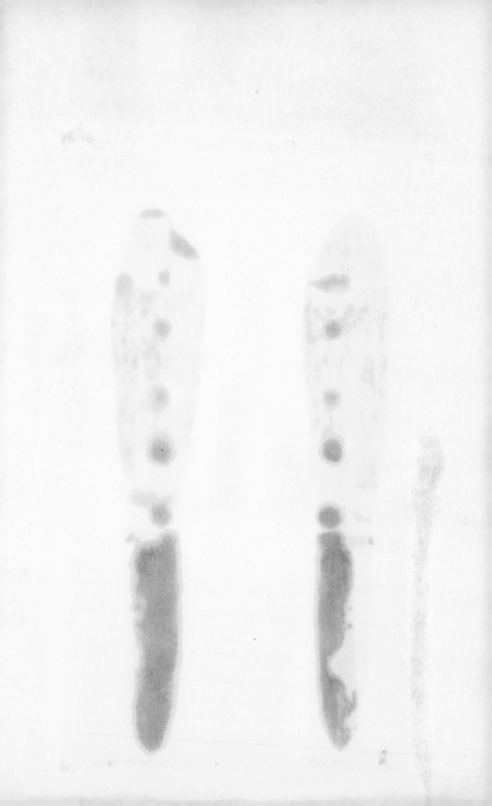